What Earth Is a Spiritual Journey?

SHERYL FURNESS

FUZZY FLAMINGO

I dedicate this book to you and every other human on Earth, my fellow conscious beings, we are all interconnected, we are all one.

I am grateful for my friends and family who have supported my own spiritual journey and writing this book. Those that have been there for me and given me inspiration, encouragement and believed in me.

Contents

Introduction
About the Author

I'm Sheryl, a thirty-six-year-old woman, working a nine-to-five job with two children and my partner. I'm a holistic therapist, offering sessions such as crystal and sound healing through my business Spiritual Dreams Crystals. I am a meditation teacher and teach the practice in meditation classes. I'll tell you more about myself in my first chapter "My Journey" and how I got into using spiritual practices. But I'd just like you to remember, I'm just your average 'girl next door' kind of woman, perhaps like you, with questions about our world; who are we, where did we come from, where do we go when we die, how do we live our lives in a spiritual way?

So, I'd like to share with you my knowledge, and I want to show you how these practices have changed me, my life, the way I deal with negative occurrences, how I use the Law of Attraction and suchlike to my advantage, how I tap in and utilise these tools and allow myself to be a spiritual being in our human existence. I now want to share them with you and with anyone who wants to listen.

I'm not completely woo-woo or a 'hippy' (although others may not agree), nor would I try to make you turn into something you don't want to be or force any practice upon you. I'm really not like that, we are all different, and everyone has their own views and opinions on all matters, not just spirituality. With spirituality, there's not a 'one box fits all'.

Recently, I have noticed a big shift in spirituality; so many people are being enlightened and looking for spiritual guidance, but don't know where to start, what to do or even *what* they are looking for. People are looking to become more mindful due to increasing stress and pace of modern life, especially since the COVID-19 lockdown period, I see more people turning to spiritual practices to help with stress, anxiety and fears and they are questioning life, our existence and ways of living. I have written this book for people who want to start living their life in a more spiritual way, for those of you who have questions but not sure where to go, this book gives you the practices and teachings that you can experiment with and, of course, research deeper if you so choose.

I truly believe that in the future spirituality will become more prevalent; people will know from birth that they are spiritual beings living a human existence. We will be taught meditation at home and school, be more in tune with ourselves, nature and the Universe and have the knowledge and understanding around things like the Law of Attraction, how to use our intuition and how to lead a life on this Earth.

As you read on through this book, you will see I will express my opinion about spirituality in *my* own words and from spiritual teachers. Spirituality is so vast, it means different things to people. Spirituality to me means having a belief about something beyond the physical world, seeing the reality of our existence outside the context that we are are conditioned to live in, learning to live your life with more awareness, presence in each moment, finding your true inner being, showing compassion towards others and having gratitude for everything in life.

CHAPTER 1

What on Earth Is a Spiritual Journey?

I'm hoping you will progress your learning as you read through this book and I take you on your *own* spiritual journey. Maybe this is your first starting point, and if it is, just by picking up this book know you have already started; you're thinking there's more to life on Earth, and that is the beginning. I feel there has been a shift in current times on spirituality, it's becoming more prevalent, and I've seen a lot of celebrities speaking out about spiritual practices; Oprah Winfrey, Russell Brand, Fearne Cotton, Holly Willoughby to name a few. There seems to be a spiritual evolution, an awakening occurring, a kind of collective consciousness that is forming in the ether and people are tapping into it, questioning spirituality, themselves, us as human beings and everything they have ever known.

Everyone has a different take on spirituality and what spirituality actually is; what should/shouldn't I do? What should I believe? Do I make spells? What is a ritual? Do

I meditate by the moon? Do I need to go to church? Do I have to turn to Buddhism? It can all be a little baffling on what to do and where to start. To be truthful, there is no right or wrong answer here, there are no set guidelines of what you must and must not do, everyone can have their own unique spiritual journey.

When researching for this book, I asked people what they thought being spiritual meant, and the answers intrigued me. A lot said the words peace, calm, energy, love, acceptance and happiness came to mind, which was interesting. Others said, "Being true to yourself and others", "Home, the place we all come from originally and where we will meet everyone again, the connections that can never be broken". I agree with all statements, however being calm is not something most humans can be 100% of the time, but this isn't a false statement. Spiritual practices can bring you calm, peace, love and acceptance, learning to connect to ourselves, finding our true inner self and being kind, compassionate to others, a more mindful approach to everyday life, because most of us can't stop our daily lives to sit in meditation all day like the Tibetan monks (I wish!).

To me, being spiritual is having a belief that there is something more to the physical realm, whether that be a sixth sense, a knowing, an experience, whatever it is, just knowing that there is something more. Having interconnectedness, oneness with all, unconditional love, finding your true inner self, knowing and understanding your true self. Having a greater connection to nature and our planet, and seeing things as they truly are. So, this book is *my* spiritual journey and *my* understanding written in *my* own words from teachings I have learnt and heard or read about, with practices that resonate with me. I hope you enjoy as I take you through some of the practices I believe in. Other people out there will have their own unique journeys, of course, with different practices, teachings and beliefs. Again, there is, in my opinion, no right or wrong teachings to follow, but a whole world of spirituality to dive into and take out of it what you enjoy and what makes you feel good. That's the main part of it, to do "what makes you feel good" and what works for you. To understand yourself on a much deeper level, to understand the real you and realise just how powerful you are.

There are so many different aspects of spiritual teachings, what to do, when to do it, how to do it. Sometimes my mind is boggled and I'm so overwhelmed by the extreme number of teachings, if I listened to them all then I'd do nothing more in my day than spiritual practices: wake up, set intentions, meditate, practise yoga, choose crystals and give them intentions, say positive affirmations, cast spells, practise Shamanic drumming, listen to a sound bath, connect to spirits, talk to angels and guides, draw angel/tarot cards, manifest desires, moon spells, practise Buddhism, if you fancy someone, throw a coin at them, say I love you and fall at their feet and they will fall in love with you. OK, so the last one is made up, but hey, why not! Wow, sometimes it's just too much of an overwhelming plethora of practices out there!

But who says these ways are correct or incorrect? Humans have made up so many teachings and rituals, whether this is developed from ancient times, passed down through centuries of teachings, with many of them becoming distorted, of course, or from modern times where we can bring some of these ancient concepts into our daily experiences or amend them to fit in with our modern lives. Some people believe their way is the only correct way, while others allow the delving in and out of practices to see which suits them. I am, of course, the latter of these.

On social media platforms, I'm constantly getting sponsored links for spiritual practices, clearly the algorithms are working! But sometimes it can feel a little daunting, in the fact that I don't practice what others do and then I start to think I should be, shouldn't I? Why don't I do that? I need to do that! Don't I? But when I delve further in, a lot is repetitive, or put in a different format. My inner guidance is that we are all energy, humans have made up these practices to help us guide our spirit and help us live better and have a clearer spiritual understanding (and a lot come back to the Law of Attraction, but let's talk about that later too!).

So, I'd like to share a few practices that I do before I go into more detail in further chapters.

- I wake up and set my affirmation for the day: "Today is going to be a great day" is my favourite mantra, or if something is happening that day then I set a good intention for it.

- I take a shower and just for a few moments I imagine all the negativity washing away from my body as the water cascades over me. I ensure I'm totally present and my mind is still.

- I choose my crystals for the day, just by looking at my personal selection and picking two or three that take my fancy, going on instinct for the day. I usually know why I've been drawn to them and then I set the intention for what I want the crystal to help me with, e.g. positive energy, grounding, speaking/communication, confidence, calming energy, determination, personal drive, building love, joyful energy to name but a few.

- I practise energy balance exercises by Donna Eden and using Qi Gong. For those who don't know, Donna is among the world's most joyous spokespersons for Energy Medicine. Her abilities as a healer are legendary; she has taught more than 100,000 people worldwide to understand the body as an energy system and to heal the body. This is a routine to help rebalance your energy system.

- I do meditation throughout my day, usually ten minutes or so here and there and a lengthier one later in the evening. As my practice has continued over the past couple of years, I find myself meditating automatically throughout the day; it's learning about when your mind needs to just stop and meditate to get you out of that build-up of thoughts when it gets too much.

- I practise mindfulness throughout the day; when I'm eating, when I'm walking, when I'm driving, having an awareness of what I'm doing in the moment. Being mindful of how I feel throughout the day and knowing when I need to stop the constant chatter in my brain and just close my eyes and meditate.
- I say my gratitude each evening, and again it comes naturally to me throughout the day now, being grateful for everything I have in my life. I usually pick three things each evening and then put my focus into one of these as I sit and think about how grateful I am, again more of this in further chapters!

So, there's a few of my daily rituals. I do not limit my practices to those above, I also do other practices ad hoc, such as specific intention setting, crystal and sound healing, moon meditation/spells, connection to guides/spirits, angel cards, but not every day, we all have busy lives, so don't get bogged down with remembering to do all your new spiritual practices, give yourself some credit!

My advice is to just see what's out there; try not to get bombarded with them all but take a few that you feel drawn to and comfortable with and go with the flow, see where they take you. Don't worry about what everyone else is doing, this is your own personal journey, you can do whatever you please. Use the exercises to help deepen your spiritual path, modify them and make them part of your ongoing practice, make your spirituality unique to you!

6

Remember to accept yourself completely in your spiritual growth, appreciate everything and let go of expectations.

So, let's delve into some practices, make your own mind up of what you feel you can relate to, what you are comfortable with, what you want to take out of this to make it your own journey.

CHAPTER 2

My Journey

I haven't got one of those stories that a lot of spiritual teachers tell you about seeing spirits as a child or rituals they practised when growing up, how they have always seen spirits and communicated and been told they are gifted. However, I do remember something, being around eight years old. I was out playing in my front garden, and I remember thinking, "I know someone up there (heaven) can hear my thoughts, and if I think good things, they will happen, and if I think bad things, they will happen." I don't know where the "voice" came from, and my parents didn't practise any spiritual practices, or know about the Law of Attraction, but it's something I used to think and just knew, without knowing anything about the Universe, Law of Attraction and vibrational energy. I knew there was a lady who looked over me, I always knew she was there to help me, guide me, I suppose, but I never had any interaction with her, I just knew she was there. So that's about all I have from being a child with regards to a spiritual side. This lady I now believe is my spirit guide. I often wonder what life would have been like if someone on our physical planet taught me about spirituality at that young age and helped me to develop and listen to my guides, my inner voice of guidance and intuition, oh think of the possibilities! If only I knew then what I know now, so the old saying goes!

It wasn't until my mother passed away after battling cancer when I was sixteen when I started wondering about spirit, where my mum had gone to. I used to think 'she can't have just disappeared'. It was a really tough time losing my mum. I had left school and was starting my working life as an admin apprentice. I can remember the day like it was yesterday, from being woken up by my auntie one cold November morning (9th November 2001), I remember how the day unfolded, not quite sure why my family were at my house so early in the morning. I don't even think I questioned it, but at that age you don't actually think, or I didn't, that my mother was about to die. I remember ringing my boss at work to explain I wasn't coming in, I remember driving up to the hospital and asking my dad what magazines she would like taking in, as this is what we had done in the past. I remember walking into the hospital room and seeing my mum, asleep, with huge apparatus around her with tubes helping her breathe. I took one look and it wasn't what I was expecting to see, so I ran out of the room. I remember my auntie following me and calming me down as I sat in another room. I went back in to see her and held her hand and said, "It's me, Sheryl." We then left and I remember coming home and going upstairs to get the photo albums out, as we sat looking through them in the living room with my aunties, uncles, grandma and grandad; I am never quite sure why my intuition told me to get the photo albums out.

My dad was upstairs, the phone rang and I went to get it, shouting upstairs, "Dad, there's a woman on the phone from the hospital for you," not having a clue what was coming next; even with my family round, it was the most unexpected thing, for me, to ever to happen. As my dad walked into the living room, taking a deep breath in, he said in a quiet voice, "Sue has passed away." I just stared at him as the words struck me like a knife and those words started to sink in… What? What did he just say? Did I hear him right, does passed away mean she's died? No… this really can't be, they've made a mistake, I don't understand, what's going on? All these words were circling my head in that split few seconds as I left the room and I ran upstairs, opened my curtains and stared out at the blue sky, looking at the clouds and thinking, where has she gone? Has she gone up there? Is there a heaven? Remember, at the time I was only sixteen, I had only known of a couple of people who had died and, being a teenager, didn't have a true understanding of life and death.

For the next week or so, I don't remember how long, perhaps it was even a couple of months, I thought they had it wrong, the nurse had made a mistake. I thought she was going to come back home and walk through the front door any moment. It was such a surreal time.

A few years later, still feeling the loss and craving to communicate with my mum, just anything to let me know she was still around (spiritually), to know she had gone *somewhere*, and just to be assured she was OK, I decided to seek out spiritualists, clairvoyants and psychic mediums. I wanted to find out how she was, where she was. But again, at that age, I had such little understanding of death from what I knew then to what I know now. I visited many over the next fifteen years. I never told any of them that I was there to receive a message from my mum, that would make me sceptical, so I sat and listened to what they had to tell me. Only one brought my mum through without me telling them first. I went to see him with my friend as I'd heard really good things about him. I always got nervous as I travelled to see a medium, with knots in my stomach and anticipation of what I was going to be told from a complete stranger. But, on this occasion, as we walked in, it was a calming experience. I went first and sat in front of him. He took my hand and started talking straight away. "You have two parents, one is in spirit… it's your mum, she's well, you look like her…" and he continued on. He knew how she passed, and also said, "At the end you were with her, you held her hand, she knew you were there." Wow, I was blown away, this person who didn't know me at all, not even my name, as it was a friend who booked my appointment and I just turned up, he knew it all, everything he said was correct, I was blown away.

On another occasion, I had gone to see a psychic medium with my sister. She went first and had informed said medium that our mum had passed, so this time I wasn't as blown away or convinced by what she had to tell me. She spoke some truths about my mum, but other things were neither true nor false, and some could have been said to anyone who had lost their mum, one of which was that I had my mum's jewellery; yes, that is quite common to have her jewellery passed down. So, I sat eagerly waiting for something, some form of truth to make me believe she was there and the lady in front of me was actually channelling her energy and bringing her here. *Come on, give me something!* The spiritualist then said, "Hmmm... there's something about a piece of jewellery, though, the ring." As she tried to bring the message through, I sat in anticipation, wondering what she would say. "The ring is missing, isn't it?" I nodded and waited for her next reply. "Don't worry, my love," she said, "I know where it is, your mum is showing me... hang on... It's in the washing machine."

I said, "Yes I lost the ring, but it's not there, I've looked, I've searched everywhere."

She said, "It is in your washing machine, your mum is telling me." We finished the rest of the reading and I went home.

I went inside and straight away looked in the washing machine; the ring wasn't there. I felt disappointed and thinking I'd just been 'had', she wasn't talking to my mum at all. Later on that day, my partner had returned from work and I retold my day, about the medium and what she had said. I went outside to the garden, playing with my children who were toddlers at the time, and my partner came out to the garden and threw an object to me, saying, "Here!" And, as I caught it, you would not believe it, it was my mum's ring, I was flabbergasted. "Oh my goodness, where did you find it?"

"It was in the washing machine, in the filter at the bottom, I popped it open and it fell out."

Wow, I couldn't believe it. I messaged the spiritualist lady saying I had found it and it was in the washing machine. She messaged a reply saying, "Don't thank me, it was your mum who told me." I sat all day thinking about my mum and thanking her and thought again about everything I had been told by this lady.

★★★

My real deeper spiritual adventure didn't start until 2016, which isn't really all that long ago. I have always had a spiritual side and over the years pondered about the Universe, why we are here; *there must be more*. It was mainly the connecting with spirit side that intrigued me the most. At this point, I hadn't heard of crystal healing, Reiki or vibrational energy, these were things picked up later along the way. But I have always had a very intuitive side, I've always known things, or been able to 'read' people, and trust my gut instinct to guide me, which has too developed with my spiritual journey.

In August 2016, I bought a book called *Earth Angel*, and I enjoyed reading Ross Bartlett's story about his spiritual journey. I went on to buy his second book about connecting to spirit and quantum physics, which I read in December 2016. After reading both books, I joined Ross's Facebook page and not long after joining he had advertised a Spiritual Development Course, which was a two-day course in Southampton. *Wow, I would love to do that*, I thought. I usually don't take myself out of my comfort zone, or I didn't back then, but this was something I really wanted to do. Getting on a train on my own all the way to Southampton to this workshop on my own and not knowing anyone or what I was about to embark on was a scary thought. But, with encouragement from my partner, I decided to do it, venture out into the big world on my own little adventure. Wow, this was exciting and nerve-racking all at the same time. What would I encounter on this journey?

I decided to stay with my sister who lived in London the day before the course, so I took the train down and stayed for the day and night. During the day, I visited Camden Market, which is one of my favourite places to go; I love the quirky shops, the street food, the atmosphere. It's amazing, with lots of spiritual gift shops. One drew my attention; a small crystal shop, and as I walked in, the lady owner sitting by her till, I gazed around and only one item caught my eye. I had no idea back then what crystals were, I had heard of them but knew nothing about them. The lady asked me, "Is there anything you like?" I pointed to a heart-shaped necklace I had seen as I walked in and asked to buy it. She brought the necklace down from the display and I purchased it. I asked her what 'fluorite' meant, as this was on the sign underneath it, and she replied, "Fluorite is for spiritual development."

I said, "Wow, I never, I'm going on a spiritual development course tomorrow!"

She replied, "Ah, you see, the crystal called out to you." I thanked her and left, thinking what on Earth is she on about, the crystal called out to me? She must be coo coo! Later, I learned that crystals do *actually* call out to you, but this comes later in the crystal chapter!

And so, my journey began from London to Southampton with only myself and my travel suitcase, as I walked up to a large, magnificent house with a beautiful well-maintained garden and knocked on the door. I was so nervous, with knots in my stomach, wondering what I was about to embark on, had I made the right decision? I was greeted and shown up to where we were going to spend the next two days, as I said hello to some of the other course participants; a mix of male and female. I sat down next to a lovely young lady who looked as nervous as me. We got chatting about how we ended up on the course and I began to relax; it seemed we were both a bit dubious about what we were going to be doing. There were eight of us in total, so it was a nice intimate group.

The first day was spent doing meditation, which was the first time I'd ever tried to do it. We began by sitting cross-legged on the floor while Ross delivered a breathing meditation; it was rather relaxing, although my mind kept wandering and I felt like I had to keep bringing myself back to the practice. Later, I learned, as I furthered my meditation practice, this is completely normal, especially for beginners. But I managed quite well considering it was my first time. We also did some candle meditation, staring at the flickering flame, which I didn't like as much; my eyes became watery and strained, and I can tell you, I haven't practised this technique since! Ross spoke to us about his book and how to connect to spirit, looking at the physics behind it. A lot of it went over my head, but I did pick up some interesting theory. We learnt how to read tarot/angel cards, which was fun, using our intuitiveness to give each other a reading. Again, this was the first time I'd even looked at angel/tarot cards and I managed to pick up some messages from spirit, which was interesting. As I felt my intuitiveness begin to flow, my guidance was telling me the lady in front of me was feeling lost in her ways. I picked up she had lost a child just by looking at the card. I didn't know where this was coming from and I was anxious about relaying to her what I was bringing through. What if she hasn't lost a child and she'll think I'm rubbish at this? But on the other hand, what if she has lost a child and she begins to get emotional? These questions were circling my mind for a few moments, but I just knew I had to tell her what I was picking up from reading the card, and yes for those of you wondering now, I was accurate. Of course, we were in a safe environment to practice in.

During the workshop, we did a small part on crystals. My first thoughts were 'what are these peculiar, intriguing-looking things, I like them!' As they were passed around one at a time, I enjoyed feeling them in my hands and I was drawn to the colours; reds, oranges, pinks, purples and blacks. Ross spoke about how he puts them under his pillow at night, saying he carries them around in his pockets and uses them to meditate with. Very intriguing, but we didn't go into any depth about them. From that moment, as I clutched my heart-shaped fluorite necklace in my hand, I knew I wanted to work with these beautiful objects of the Earth and little did I know where my adventure would take me!

And that brings me on to my next adventure, crystal healing. I did some research when I returned home, internet research and buying crystal books, and then went on to do a diploma course on crystals, where I found out more exciting information, gaining a deeper knowledge, learning about the energy field and the properties of crystals, the vibrational energy and how crystals can help to heal all aspect of one's life, and this became the birth of Spiritual Dreams Crystals, my new adventure.

CHAPTER 3

A Soul Within a Physical Body

We weren't put on this Earth to work forty hours a week, surely this isn't it; to be born, become a toddler learning about the world and how to interact, go to pre-school/nursery, go to school for fourteen years, go to college/university or further education, get a job and work until we are sixty-five (or more)! I ask myself this question and ponder on it quite a lot. With all life's systems that are put in place for us, are we really free beings in our physical world? I always think of our typical lives, getting up every day and doing the same routine; breakfast, coffee, working all day (because we have to get paid, right?), journey back home, seeing to the kids, cooking, cleaning, reading, watching TV and going back to bed so we can do it all again tomorrow. Yes, routine can bring us stability and the ability to manage daily life, but if you could choose how to live your life, would you choose to do this? You know there is more to life than that! We are conditioned to sleep for eight hours (as a rough guide) and eat three meals a day, now what if we lived freely, napped when you wanted (oh the joy!), stayed up till you wanted and woke up when you wanted, without that damn alarm clock that humans brought into existence, oh, how different life would be!

On average, we spend approximately forty hours going to work to earn a living each week, the majority of people doing a job they don't like or can't find a way out of, making them stressed day in, day out, and even when we aren't working we are still thinking about our jobs, our careers. And yes, we must live a working life to get by in this world, which us humans created for ourselves, in order to have structure and money that was brought into our existence. Money was created by humans who gave these notes and coins their monetary worth so we could buy items that we need to live; food, shelter, warmth. Therefore, we have to earn money, working being the main way to do so, and so the cycle continues; work, earn money, spend money, work, earn money, spend money. Plus, it was a way for the government to keep us in order, provide structure and an economy, and to segregate class; the rich from the poor, but let's not get into all of that in this book! People believe you need money to be happy and successful, and yes money can buy things that make us momentarily happy, but remember peace and happiness come from within us. No wonder so many people are unhappy, depressed and feeling like they have to strive for success. Being successful is what we believe we should be doing; we are told to strive for it and feel like a failure if we aren't successful and rich. But in all of this, our spiritual awakening, our journey, our soul's purpose can't be fully achieved as our life as we know it stands in the way of us being able to fully see the bigger picture, of life, its purpose, our true self and why we are here on this planet living as a human being.

We are conscious beings inside a human body, we are souls having a human experience. I like the example I once heard, it goes a little something like this: There once was a girl who lived in a faraway land, in a beautiful and peaceful village; everyone was connected and carefree, it was pure joy, no worries, no stress, no war, just peace. There was a wise elder man who helped the villagers there, giving them direction and guidance and they all lived in harmony. He often talked about the 'other place'. One day the girl approached the wise elder man and asked, "What is the purpose of this life?" He decided to show her, and that evening they held a ceremony. The girl lay in the centre on an altar as all the villagers gathered around her chanting. The girl closed her eyes as she saw a bright white light. As she left her body, she could see all her connected beings below her. As the light took her up, she could hear the chanting becoming fainter and fainter to just a light mumble, then to nothing. It became dark as she continued floating effortlessly, bodiless, into a dark entity. Everything was forgotten, she didn't have a memory, all she could see was darkness. She suddenly felt forced towards a pinpoint of white light, as she made her way towards the light and into a brand new world. She was born, a human child, in the waking (or should we say unwoken) world, her thoughts and memories gone. She could see blurry figures and let out a scream, she was cradled, and this was the birth of her human life. She wouldn't see her spirit family until her death. As humans, we seek to become spirit, striving towards a spiritual ideal, and as souls we seek to become human to experience a physical reality.

I read a book called *Journey of Souls* by Michael Newton, which has stayed with me and my beliefs of the after death existence. He is a hypnotist and hypnotises his clients into a deep state where they see their soul's in-between lives, in-between their reincarnations on Earth. It describes each case study and what was relayed back as he asks questions on where they go after they die, who meets us when we die and what the spirit world is. Surprisingly, or not, each case study had very similar experiences and it really intrigued me. Under his hypnosis, his clients would go into the hypnotic state and Michael would begin asking questions. Their replies were of a similar nature; they would see themselves in their previous life in human form, they would describe the scene around them and get to a point where their death was upon them, knowing they were about to die. As they took their last breath, they would feel peace, this peaceful harmony wash over them, as they began to leave their physical body, as if they were hovering above themselves, watching the scene below them as loved ones cradled them. They were then greeted with other spiritual beings, sometimes people they recognised or had a familiar connection with. They would then, bodiless, be floating as energy into a black hole and eventually reach another realm. In this other realm there are what are called 'levels' of consciousness, where they would learn and be taught, preparing them for another human existence.

Albert Einstein proved that all the energy of the Universe is constant and that it can neither be created nor destroyed. It is my belief that once we die our soul leaves our physical body, our energy merges with other souls' energy, where we meet our spirit family (once again), allowing us to grow and progress in the spirit world and have the opportunity to be reincarnated into a human form again. But there are still so many unanswered questions: Is there another realm? Can we prove it? Can we take our mind back into previous lives? Is part of our old life's consciousness within us in our current physical form? Can we be reincarnated? What does the spirit world look like?

Humans are conditioned as soon as we are born into the world, meaning we don't live life as freely as we want. We are disconnected with spirituality and allow our personal being to be controlled with systems. Of course, a lot of systems are positive, take for example the justice system. Imagine a world without policing! The world would become utter chaos. But we are conditioned to live in society and act and behave like everyone else from the moment we are born; we are told fictional stories about how we should behave, how we should see the world, how we should follow religions and teachings, follow set rules, how we should live our lives. You may be thinking, no I'm not conditioned, I do what I please, but when you think about it on a deeper level, do you go to bed every night at the same time, do you eat three set meals a day, do you always go for your lunch at midday, do you work in a job that doesn't bring you happiness, do you do the same things day in day out, doing the same as everyone else, only believe in a certain way and not allow your mind to expand? All this is created and taught by us humans, everything that is told to us is a story that a human or group of humans believed and taught to the masses. When everyone believes this and follows it, it is then seen as 'society norms'. You could say religion plays a part in this too.

> *"If only our eyes saw souls instead of bodies, how very different our ideas of beauty would be."*
>
> ~ *Unknown*

I love this saying and how very true it is, if only we could see our connections, our souls, our loving beings, our true inner selves instead of the shell we live in, how different our world would be and how different we would view people and the world we live in. We don't have to be the skinniest, the prettiest, the fittest, have the most money, be able to buy the best house/holidays/cars; really we don't have to be. I am going to put some of the blame on social media in this modern time. People believe you have to look a certain way and to be the best, to have the most, have the most followers on social media, the most likes on your posts, the best holidays, the most expensive car. If only we could see our souls and realise we don't need these materialistic things or to be those things.

If someone does something 'out of the norm', people describe it as weird or different, as we are all conditioned to have tunnel vision in this society with how to think, act and behave. Even in different parts of the world, or as closely as different cities in the country and even closer within different social groups in the same area. People will say, for example, 'Look what she's done to her hair.' 'Can you believe what she is wearing?' 'He wants to go run off and live in a tent in the middle of a deserted forest and build his own life, that is crazy!' Why do we believe people expressing how they want to be and live their life that is different to how we live ours, is absurd? As I've matured – I honestly have, don't laugh – and also as a part of my spiritual development, I'm starting to 'not give a sh★t', pardon my language, of what people think. If I want to go and live in a tree house in the middle of the forest with my pink hair and harem pants, and be an outsider to the money-hungry world of business, then I very well shall, my friends; this is my journey and I am not bothered by your opinion! If only we all had this approach from being young, imagine what we could have become without worrying about what people may think of us and not having to be forced to live the social norms.

Take, for example, LGBTQ+: it is human nature to fall into being attracted to the opposite and also the same sex, even animals are gay! But humans, back in BC times where it was written to say man should not sleep with man, created this 'rule' and, of course, back in those times they believed that there would be a lack of offspring, so created a rule that the people should follow. But this belief, as it filtered through generations and distorted and disentangled from its original interpretations, became a thing, it became known that this was 'wrong' because of something a group of people decided thousands of years ago. Over the past twenty years or so it has become more acceptable in society, after all this time, can you believe it, and I say *more acceptable* and not *accepted*, as still to this day there is homophobic abuse, there are countries where same-sex couples can't be married, and it was only 2013 in the UK when Parliament passed the Marriage (Same-Sex Couples) Act, which introduced civil marriage for same-sex couples in England and Wales. There are still countries in this world that arrest and even murder people for being gay and all because of this one rule that was made up thousands of years ago by a person, or group of people, and was so ingrained that people believed it to be true and still do.

Other rules or beliefs include marriage; some people wish to get married, others don't, but the ones who don't are always questioned, 'When are you going to get married?' 'Why aren't you married?' as if it's absolutely necessary this must be achieved at some point in your life, and that it should be achieved in your twenties. Again, religion plays a part in this and the belief that this is a must for everyone. Going back in history through centuries, girls would get married at a very young age, usually because life spans weren't as long as they are nowadays, and a lot died from childbirth or from infectious disease such as influenza and tuberculosis. Rather than waiting to find someone they could fall in love with, girls were paired up with boys and forced or encouraged to be married and bear children at an early age. And I bet most weren't in happy relationships, were there even 'happy' relationships in those days? As we move on through time to the present, although this still does go on, people now have more choice, especially with the introduction of the internet, no longer can you only find someone who lives within a couple of miles of you, the whole world is now your oyster! But even still, people should wait until they find true love, the person they truly want to be with before jumping into marriage, not because they feel it's what they should do, or perhaps they may actually decide that they don't want to get married at all, why should we judge that, why should everyone be 'sheep' and follow suit just because everyone else does it? I'll leave that question there for you to ponder on, not just on the marriage front but on everything.

The Ego

Our ego is a thought form, it's a form of how we identify ourselves, who we see ourselves as. The ego is a self-concept, identifying ourselves through our own thoughts and emotions and a lot of it isn't our true reality. We are filled with misconceptions about who we actually are.

We believe that voice inside our head, 'I'm a failure', 'I'm never going to be able to achieve', 'I look ugly'. We let these thoughts that pop into our mind dictate our lives and tell us who we think we are. The ego is often described as a phantom self as we have so many limiting beliefs. These recurring thoughts start to dictate who we *believe* we are. I love the example of animals: a dog doesn't have an ego, he doesn't have a self-image, he has no worries and doesn't have to carry the weight of his ego. It always makes me giggle thinking of a dog saying to his owner, "Sorry, Mum, I can't go out for a walk today, I look terrible." On the spiritual path, the ego can be an obstruction to our enlightenment and learning to be aware of this can be tricky to achieve. The ego is judgemental if you let it be. How many posts do you now see on social media, especially the news/press groups, the negativity in there is huge, people being argumentative, judgemental, hurtful, spiteful, it's an awful place and stemmed from people's egos, causing discomfort, losing our peace and joy by joining in with criticism. I can never understand why some people are this way, being so judgemental and hurtful towards others, but you can learn things yourself from this, on how you respond and how judging you are in others and yourself. Take an honest look within yourself to see if you share some of the characteristics you dislike in others.

> *"If we learn to open our hearts, anyone, including the people who drive us crazy, can be our teacher."*
> ~ *Pema Chodron*

As Deepak Chopra says, "This is the deepest insight in Buddhism, your true self isn't known to you as you are too busy with the other selves." He says your true self is hiding from us, your source. At the top is the ego/social self, which is wrapped up in the everyday world. The next is the private self with all its worries, fears, dreams and fantasies. The next level is the intimate self where you feel safe enough to express love, compassion, kindness, inspiration and devotion, all qualities can be expressed in a fulfilling relationship. Going deeper into your awareness, the sense of 'who I am' changes. On the surface, you think of all the things you say and do, but this is a superficial self – as you go deeper, you become more yourself; calm, quiet and centred, capable of falling in love and feeling compassion. Having a spiritual awareness and practising techniques to quieten the mind, such as doing meditation, is bringing you further towards your true self, the *real* you.

The ego prevents us from seeing our reality by deceiving us into believing we only exist materialistically. We are always *wanting*; we want happiness, we want a big house, we want the best holiday, we want the perfect partner, we want the best/ the most, we want, we want, we want. We believe we need things from external sources to make us happy. However, we are never satisfied, we always want more. Even down to small things; for example, 'I want that piece of cake', 'That piece of cake will make me so happy', 'All I want is that cake'. We then eat the cake, and yes momentarily we are enjoying the cake, perhaps we are mixing our interpretations of what happiness is with partial enjoyment, but nevertheless, we are enjoying the cake. But then we are left after eating it with feelings of wanting again, we want more, what else will now make me happy, I want more cake! You could make the same comparison to 'likes' on a social media post, craving the likes, but you see, our happiness is short-lived, we are constantly craving the next piece of happiness (the cake, more 'likes'), seeking it out. But one has to realise, and with spiritual practices such as meditation you can begin to have a true understanding, that peace and happiness comes from within, within your own self. Find that and you will have all you need, the transcendental dimension of who you are. May you never seek happiness from cake and 'likes' again!

Using spirituality and meditation, the quietening of the mind helps us to not be trapped in the mindset where the ego tells us who we are, where our focus can get *beyond* the material aspects in life, training our mind to not see from the limited perspective; for example, if you believe that people on the whole should be a certain way, then your ego will only allow you to see from that limited perspective and will bring people into your existence that validate that belief. If you want to change your ego then you need to reprogramme your beliefs. We will talk about gratitude and positive affirmations later in this book.

This is where we can start to find out how to achieve our true happiness. When you are sensing instead of thinking, for example when you are out walking and you notice something beautiful, perhaps a sunset, rainbow or beautiful scenery and you just stop for a moment and just look without the chatter of thoughts in your mind, we start to realise that who we are isn't the thoughts and emotions we have about ourselves (our ego), but instead an expansive *awareness* behind those thoughts, the witness of our inner world, and this is how to find our inner peace – our true selves.

CHAPTER 4

The World As We Know It?

Buddhists speak of "maya", translated to pretence, deceit or illusion. The Mahayana Abhidharma teachings talks about the illusion of things that appear different to what they are, making humans believe in what is actually an illusion. They believe that nothing actually exists, therefore there is nothing and our existence is an illusion.

Hinduwebsite.com explains: *"According to many schools of Hinduism, the world is an illusion, a play of the supreme consciousness of God."*

They also describe illusion; *"Illusion is appearance of things differently from what they are actually. For example, everything in the Universe is in a constant motion, but we think as if we live in a stable world because we do not perceive the motion, unless we pay particular attention to the planets and the stars and the movement of time. The sky has no colour. But to our eyes it appears as blue, because of the reflection of the light by the molecules in the air. So, you see, the illusion of things we see every day but do not acknowledge mentally.*

A simple analysis of our perceptual experience establishes beyond doubt that the world is not what it appears to be and what we perceive through our senses is just a superficial reality. Science tries to go beyond the visible Universe and unravel the truth hidden in the depths of matter. But at times it gets caught in the appearances of things and layers of complexity that is part of our analytical approach. Hindu scriptures remind us of this fact when they compare the world to an illusion. It is an illusion because it conceals truth and reveals itself differently each time we perceive it."

We are living our lives in this different perception, the world as we see it being different to what actually *is*. The world is being shown to us from how other people see it and how they want us to see it, how generations have seen it and slowly now on how science can show us. We can't see gravity, but we are told there is this force called gravity keeping everything pinned to the ground, we can't see molecules with our naked eye, but science tells us they exist, we can't see our energy field, but we can feel it.

God

I want to write a small paragraph on God and how it fits in with spirituality. God is usually pictured in art as a man on a cloud in the sky. People refer to God as a powerful being, the creator of life, this man on the cloud who created the world. Now my belief is that this picture is shown to us as we can't actually show/draw what 'God' really is. It's a metaphor, it's a descriptive picture to depict something that isn't literally true but helps explain an idea or comparison.

I believe this force, if you want to call it the word 'God', created life and energy and universal power. As science has yet to show us what the Universe is and how the Universe operates, then a man on a cloud controlling everything is how we are shown it (in Christianity), because it's what our minds can comprehend, rather than trying to explain a force. When someone dies from a terrible illness, you'll hear people saying, 'God only takes the best', or, 'How can God do this, how can He let these bad things happen to us?' Well, the man on the cloud hasn't let these bad things happen to us, these things happen because of universal forces, the Law of Attraction at work. Of course, bad (negative) occurrences happen in our world as there is negative energy around us and negative thought patterns and consciousness from us humans. I mean, how many truly positive people do you know? How much positivity is there on social media compared with negativity? The world will never be a peaceful, harmonious place as we are all far from an energetic alignment of peace. I have heard some spiritual people speak of death as being a positive experience and even going as far as to be jealous of those who die, as they believe they will transform into their souls of peace and harmony; remember the story I shared in an earlier chapter. In some ways, yes, I believe this too. Therefore, God to me means universal creation, powers beyond our physical realm, life force energy, which does merge with a lot of religious beliefs.

★★★

We are all on our own journey through life and people will only understand as much as their understanding will allow. I would never try to force someone to listen to *my way* of doing things, but rather guide people and show them an understanding, but of course only if they are ready to listen and want to know, with which they can choose to apply or ignore.

So, what on Earth is this spiritual journey I keep referring to? Well, as I've said previously, this book is *my* perspective and some people have alternative perspectives, there isn't a right or wrong answer here, it's all a matter of interpretation and it's a phrase that can be defined differently.

A spiritual journey to me means that you have an understanding that we are all made of energy and all connected to source energy, you have a spirit (soul, consciousness) and we are all connected from one. It's also about being at peace with our own individual selves in the human body we have been given, it's about the gift of life itself, finding love within our own selves, and knowing and trusting your intuition and guidance. Also, to me, the journey is about finding ways to achieve these things, achieving inner peace, for example, through meditation, connecting with nature, finding these spiritual practices to help our journey of understanding and being at one, finding joy, peace and love within ourselves, using intuition to guide us through life and knowing there is a greater life force.

Now, being spiritual doesn't mean you live your life on 'cloud nine', where everything is hunky-dory *all* the time, where nothing bad ever happens. However, it does mean that you have the tools, the mindset and guidance to help you get through and/or avoid difficult challenges. Through spiritual practices, we can respond in a more powerful way and come to a resolution easier and with less 'drama'.

Even for the most humanist in our society, there will come a time in life where you will ask an esoteric question, where no answer can be found in our physical world that sufficiently satisfies your appetite for the need to seek out something that feels right for you. This in essence is spirituality in action. We are unable to live a life where spirituality doesn't interject into one's journey somewhere along the way, in this thing called a lifetime. It will arise in everyone in a different way but will always be there. For those who declare atheism, their belief is so strong in this that it is a strand under the banner of spirituality.

> *"There are more things in heaven and earth, Horatio, than are dreamt of in your philosophy."*
>
> ~ *Hamlet*

People always ask me, "But how will I know I'm on a spiritual journey?" "What happens when I am awake?" (as some people refer to the phrase 'spiritual journey' as an awakening) and my answer to these questions is always nothing is going to happen, you don't get a badge saying you're awoken now and on your spiritual journey, congratulations! It can be a gradual process, or perhaps one day you will just wake up literally and metaphorically and it hits you in the face, what is the purpose of my existence, what is life, who am I? It's a journey, not a race, you are exactly where you need to be, it's life, we are all learning. It's all about having an understanding of life and source energy, knowing you are beyond a physical body. You will begin to trust your inner knowing and begin the process of realisation about what you thought you knew to be true, the reality that you could not see before. You are experiencing your own unique time as a physical being and will begin to see there's not a 'one box fits all', which we are sometimes expected to fit into. By this, I mean the conditioned way of life we are expected to live. Walk your own path with a deeper understanding of your true purpose, being true to yourself and not allowing others to influence your beliefs. Hindu text describes the wheel of birth and death; we will keep coming back till we are awake.

For those who ask if they are on a spiritual journey, the answer is yes, yes you are, you have asked the question and therefore you have started the journey, you are starting to have a basic understanding, and if you are reading this book then hey, guess what? You're on your own unique spiritual journey too. So, just enjoy, meditate, read, let your soul be happy and find inner peace. Spend time away from social media and spend that time exploring nature; rivers, seas, forests, beaches, watching the sun rise and set and connecting to the moon.

As you begin to delve into spirituality and cultivate spiritual practices you may find that you start to notice things; the Universe sending you messages, gentle nudges to help you on your way. I'm talking about the types of things that some people just ignore or put to one side as they don't fully understand their meaning or how or why they are happening. Just because science hasn't found out a way to confirm, it doesn't mean these forces don't exist. We just haven't been able, as humans, to put a contextual scientific explanation to label it. Perhaps you are thinking about doing something, but unsure of which path to go down, so you ask the Universe for guidance, and you may start to then notice occurrences; seeing things on the TV, hearing something on the radio that jumps out at you, or something just catches your eye, or perhaps you bump into someone who talks about the thing you are thinking about, or being recommended a book on the subject of the thing you are in two minds about. Remember to trust these signs, the Universe is showing you, telling you, and you have to trust your intuition and guidance to act upon it.

You may notice 'coincidences', but in my view, there is no such thing as a coincidence. What people refer to as coincidences, I believe are occurring because of the

Law of Attraction (LOA) being in force; when you think something and send those thoughts out to the Universe, with true meaning and intent, they come back to you.

"Nothing is accidental, the Universe is too intelligent for that type of creation."

~ *Spiritual League Quote*

I mean, how many times have you heard someone say 'eee, what a coincidence' or 'we were just talking about that'. You may be thinking about a person, then you bump into them at the supermarket, and you will say, "Wow, what a coincidence, I was just thinking about you." It happens all the time. I've lost count of the number of times I've thought of someone and then they have rung or texted me at that exact moment. How many times does a thought pop into your mind, and you say it out loud and someone next to you says, "I was just going to say that." You are picking up their thought energy, as our thoughts are energy too; you're tapping into the thought energy around you. This tends to become more frequent as you become more spiritually aware. Coincidence or the Law of Attraction in force? I'll let you ponder on that.

"There are no accidents or coincidences in life – everything is synchronicity – because everything has a frequency. It's simply the physics of life and the Universe in action."
~ *Rhonda Byrne, The Power*

A lot of people aren't aware of the LOA, or choose not to believe in these 'forces', but those who *are* aware can use it in their everyday life. Again, I'm not going to preach to anyone or try and make people understand; if they want to listen then I will share my knowledge, if they don't then that is their choice. The LOA is continually working at all times, even when we aren't consciously aware of it or if we believe in it or not.

As you work on your spiritual practice, you may notice your intuition becoming stronger. We all have intuitive abilities, it's that gut instinct feeling, something you just know without any reason, you just 'know' if something is a good idea or a bad idea, you know events are going to happen before they come about. Intuition is a tool that we can choose whether or not to develop. Some people are easily able to tap into it, and some can't sense it at all. As you become more in tune, you start understanding these feelings, sensing things, noticing how information comes to you, and being guided intuitively by your spirit guides to develop a more pronounced level of intuition and understanding.

This can lead to other abilities, in the sense of psychic and clairvoyant abilities. A psychic can predict things that will happen in the future, whereas a medium who is clairvoyant (can see images in the mind), clairaudience (can hear voices in the mind), clairsentient (can recognise feelings, gut instincts, sense energy) or claircognizance (is inner knowing) can hear, see, feel, know information and speak to what we call spirits of people who have passed away. Again, everyone has this ability if they tap into it. I often have people say, "I've been told I have the gift," but anyone can use and develop this ability, you just have to have time and patience to develop it. Some people may feel a stronger connection in one area alone, and others can tap into all four clairs.

"Eventually you will stop calling them coincidences, and realise just how powerful you are."

~ *Unknown*

CHAPTER 5

Energy

"Everything is energy and that's all there is to it. This is not philosophy. This is physics."

~ Albert Einstein

Again, energy is something people can't see so don't acknowledge it or don't understand its existence, it is inaccessible to us. I believe there is a world beyond our senses, and we are limited in what we can see and hear, for example particles and frequencies that surround us. As we can't see them, we can't believe they are tangible. We forget that our Universe where our planet Earth is, is like a tiny speck of dust in comparison to the expansive Universes out there, it's sometimes difficult for us as humans to comprehend and we don't give it much thought.

There are things that happen out there that to us seem like magic and are unexplainable in our reality, like coincidences or knowing things that are going to happen, or on another level seeing spirits/ghosts and even UFOs. I do believe that ghosts are an imprint of energy that keeps recurring, which is why people claim to see the same 'ghost' doing the same thing, for example walking the same corridor. I believe there is a greater consciousness that surrounds us with super physical forces. Just because something cannot necessarily be tangibly measured does not mean that it does not exist. Intuition and energy in the form of vibration have a harder task to submit to the limited boundaries of our current science and quantitative structure. However, there can be found good qualitative studies. For example, although we cannot experience it, we now hold as common knowledge derived from studies that dogs can hear four times further than humans. Also, many a reference has been made to the sixth sense.

Biofield is a theory that describes the electromagnetic field that surrounds every living being. According to Ann L. Baldwin, PhD, a Reiki researcher, the heart produces an electric field, using an electrocardiogram (ECG) to monitor heartbeats, the brain also has an electrical field. All cells produce an electrical charge through positive and negative charges, creating magnetic fields. The interference pattern between two human magnetic fields may explain some of the results that *any* touch therapy creates. The theory of quantum physics may hold promise in the future explanation of the mechanisms of Reiki.

In the 1990s, Dr. John Zimmerman was able to measure a biomagnetic field coming from a healing practitioner's hands with a device called a superconducting quantum interference device (SQUID). A few years later a Japanese team measured a biomagnetic field emanating from the hands of practitioners of yoga, meditation, Qigong and similar modalities. Information on the study can be found at the back of this book.

I do like to have tangible evidence on how things work, but sometimes I just think, if something works for you, then it just works, and do you really need to know all the intricacies? Although, science is now catching up to prove some of these.

Everything is made out of vibrational energy, your thoughts are energy, every thought leaves your body into the Universe, merging with other thought energy. Inside each one of our cells, molecules vibrate. If you could see your body energetically with your eyes, you would see it as vibrational pulsating colours of light. Once we tune into our energy, we can connect with ourselves and others on a more profound level and this in turn can help improve our emotional, physical and spiritual well-being. The more you understand yourself as an energy system and the deeper you take this, the easier it is to navigate around situations, you know when and when not to invest your energy. As you ascend your energy from survival towards enlightenment, your perceptions change, and your mindfulness enhances.

When an entire society thinks the same way, their thoughts produce their reality. If they think and live in fear, then fear will become part of their reality. Similarly, people can produce high positive energy, if their thoughts are strong enough they can produce great results. Thought is creative.

So, let's talk about vibrational energy. For example, if you are feeling excited, enthusiastic, passionate, happy, joyful, have lots of confidence, motivation, determination, drive, you're appreciative, have abundance, then your energy is vibrating at a *high* frequency. However, on the other hand, if you are feeling bored, anxious, stressed out, angry, resentful, have a lack of confidence, sluggish, sad, then you are vibrating at a *lower* frequency.

Highest	Love, joy, gratitude, passion, excitement, enlightenment, peace
High	Contentment, ease, acceptance, hope, encouragement, courage, confidence
Low	Impatient, frustrated, bored, doubtful, worry, anxiety, judgemental
Lowest	Fear, anger, hatred, guilt, shame, depression, despair, grief

When you vibrate at a higher frequency you don't tend to notice the challenges in your reality and you will find yourself skipping around them. The challenges that you do face, you are able to deal with more efficiently and you come to resolutions easier, sooner and see more fulfilling results. These positive higher vibrations make us feel at ease. But, when you vibrate at the lower frequencies you are more likely to experience negativity, frequent negative situations and be more likely to feel things like frustration, annoyance, feel you're not good enough or unable to cope, that you will never achieve, feeling more stress and anxiety. You may then start to accumulate what energy healers call 'a blockage' within the energy field; these blockages of energy cause us to vibrate at a lower frequency. Let's take the heart chakra; for example, if you have blockages around the heart chakra and it's not vibrating in tune with its natural frequency, you won't be able to feel as much joy, love and compassion. Then in turn you will start to attract more lower vibrational people, situations and things into your existence. You may not be able to show affection, you may be showing jealousy or unable to form healthy relationships. So, this is why it is important to continually raise our vibrational frequency and clear these 'blockages' in our energy field, so we start attracting higher vibrational things and situations to us and people who radiate joy, compassion, love and make us feel good, we are able to build healthier relationships and be a loving being.

You may notice energy unconsciously. Have you ever walked into a room where you suddenly feel drained, your energy drops, it doesn't feel good, there's an unpleasant atmosphere? This is because of the 'negative' energy, the low vibrating energy within the room. This energy may be from a person or group of people, it may be from someone who's been in the room prior to you, but you can feel it, sense it and it leaves you feeling drained, like an energy sucker!

You may notice when you're speaking to someone who has low vibrational energy, they may always be moaning to you and being negative about themselves or others, and this may leave you feeling drained and you may come away from a conversation with them and feel totally flummoxed, sluggish and in a 'can't be bothered' mood. They have literally sucked the good energy from you and left you with low vibrational energy, and you must then pick yourself back up, get that good high vibrational energy flowing again!

You may find you dislike someone, and you're not sure why? They haven't done anything towards you, you may just not like being around them, or perhaps feel that uncomfortable feeling when you are with them. This is because they have a different vibration to yours. You attract people who give out similar vibrational energy. Therefore, sometimes you lose touch with friends as vibrational energy levels change, you grow apart, your energies vibrate to others that have your vibrational energy. 'Your vibe is your tribe' is a saying I like!

> *"As you grow spiritually, people will inevitably fall from your life because you have risen to new levels of understanding. Let them go, eventually like-minded people with a similar frequency to yours will take their place."*
>
> ~ *Quote by Children of Light*

Your energy can fluctuate depending on what's going on in your life; what people have said to you, situations you find yourself in, things you have read or seen on social media, the news channels where a lot of it is negative, even the change in weather, receiving good or bad news or thinking about our own memories. These can have a great effect on our energy and start to weaken our energetic field when we concentrate on them or feel the impact of them. It's like a tumbleweed effect, the more negativity you see and hear the more the tumbleweed of negativity begins to grow until it spirals out of control and results in our energy being so low that we suffer physically.

You might ask, but why do I need to vibrate at a high frequency? Well, not only does it make you feel good and more positive about yourself and life, going on the Law of Attraction (LOA) where 'like attracts like', if you are sending out positive energy, whatever we feel and think, we are sending those vibrational thoughts and feelings out and the Universe is receiving those vibrations, and you are then in return receiving more of them back to you.

The LOA works on whatever you are thinking and feeling because they are energy too, and so whatever you think, however you feel, you attract back to you when you are in alignment with it. We are what Esther Hicks describes us as being, "deliberate creators and as such we have the power to calibrate towards what we want to manifest in our life." So, it's good to be consciously aware of this, and ensure that you are continually sending out energy, thoughts and feelings that resonate with what you want to be, what you want to do, what you want to experience, good situations and events and how you want to feel. You don't want to send out what you don't want. Because remember, whatever vibrations you send out, you shall receive in return! When we resist something, for example when you say, "I don't want this," "I don't want to feel anxious," "I don't want this person in my life," even though you are saying you *don't* want it, because you are giving your attention to it and you're thinking about it, you're sending those vibrations out of this thing/feeling/person. The "I *don't* want" part doesn't get heard by the Universe, so you start receiving more of it back to you, and that thing you are resisting is manifesting more into your life.

Other examples of energy:

You or someone you know may always say things like:

- "I always have bad relationships, I can never keep a boyfriend/girlfriend, my partners always cheat on me."
- "I don't like my job, I hate being in this job, nothing ever goes right in this job."
- "I haven't got enough money, I never have money, I'm always broke."
- "I think I'm coming down with something, I'm always poorly."
- "He/she doesn't appreciate me, I'm always taken for granted."
- "My life is a mess, everything is always going wrong."

So, you'll probably be thinking now, yes I know someone who says one or more of those things, it may even be yourself, a friend, a partner. Even saying those phrases out aloud, I can feel that shift of vibrational energy in me, I feel a knot in my tummy, I can feel the negativity of the phrases. You'll find that these situations are continuing to be experienced by the people who say these comments; for example, "Every boyfriend I have cheats on me," and low and behold the next partner they have will also cheat on them. "This always happens to me," and true to its word, it continues to happen. They become stuck in a cycle of these negative thoughts continuing to happen. Remember the tumbleweed effect, because they are always thinking it and giving their attention to it, talking about it, building up the momentum and the LOA says back, OK you want that, I shall deliver it, there you go.

Whatever energy and thoughts you put out there you get them back, so we want to vibrate at higher frequencies, have positive energy and thoughts to attract more goodness and positivity back to us. You may have heard of the sayings, "What goes around comes around," "You get what you give," "You reap what you sow," these sayings are describing the same thing, The LOA.

You start your day, maybe you're stuck in traffic and running late for work, you start to feel the anger rising within your stomach or in your chest. Then someone pulls their car out in front of your car, and your anger intensifies, you can feel the frustration. As the momentum builds, you finally pull up at the work office late and frustrated. You get into the office and trip over, "Oh can this day get any worse?" you cuss at yourself. Again, feeling the anger and annoyance rising. You go to make your morning coffee in the office kitchen, open the cupboard and the sugar falls out, spilling across the bench. You'll keep saying in your mind, "Argh, I'm having such a day of it, everything's going wrong!!!" Then you'll start telling people in the office about your lousy morning, and guess what? This builds up the momentum too. You'll have said this phrase before, I'm sure: "I should just go back to bed and start the day again." This, ladies and gentlemen, is an example of the LOA at work. You're giving your attention to the things that are going wrong, sending out those intentions of "I want annoying" to the Universe, which are starting to build up the negative energy and you're getting more of it back. It all started with one thing, one negative thought and/or emotion. So, learning how to shift your energy is great and using positive affirmations, crystals and meditation are great ways you can do this, which we will look at in further chapters!

Learning how to become aware of your thought patterns, those negative patterns of resistance, when you say, "I don't want this," or being in that negative frame of mind is the start of knowing when you need to shift the thought pattern and come away from resisting it. Instead of saying, "I can't do this, I'm never going to be able to achieve, I'm not good enough, nothing is going right, I don't want to feel like this," instead of getting into that negative spiral, just start by acknowledging the thought and emotion. Allow the thought to be there, witness it, be aware of the thought. So, for example, if someone has annoyed you, you start getting worked up, saying, "They have annoyed me so much, I'm frustrated, I can't believe this is happening." Instead of stomping around getting all het up, simply stop and witness how you are; your emotions, your feelings, witness and be aware of the negative energy, but allow it, and then let it dissipate, let it go. Now I know it's easier said than done, but once you have acknowledged you're in this negative state, you can then begin to shift your vibrational energy, you can choose how you want to think and feel, what could make you feel one step closer to peace? How do you want the situation to progress? How do you really want to feel? You could think about a time that made you happy, remembering and picturing that time in your mind, reliving those happy emotions, how you felt. You could change your thoughts to look at how you want the situation to look like, play out a more positive outcome in your mind. In that moment that you bring your attention to what you want, the negative attraction will stop, and the positive attraction will begin. Remember the 'problem' in this case, the person who has made you annoyed, well they will still be there, the situation hasn't changed, but it's how you *choose* to deal with it, how you choose to let your mind take over it, how you choose what you want the LOA to bring into your existence.

Your thoughts create feelings, your feelings create actions, and your actions create your situations and events. Choose how you want to feel, choose your events and make them a positive experience for yourself.

★★★

In an earlier chapter I referred to Donna Eden and how I practise her energy balance routine. Donna Eden is an energy healer, her website describes her: "Donna is among the world's most sought, most joyous, and most authoritative spokespersons for Energy Medicine. Her abilities as a healer are legendary."

"Energy Medicine brings you vitality when you are drained, health when you are ill, and joy when you are down."

~ *Donna Eden*

I stumbled across Donna when I was looking into energy balance and I couldn't resist watching her numerous videos on YouTube. She brings such joy as she speaks and uplifted my spirits just by watching and listening to her, and my interest grew. Donna has been teaching energy balance methods for over forty years, and how to see the body as a collection of energy systems that can facilitate healing. Donna's website says: "Energy Medicine awakens energies that bring resilience, joy, and enthusiasm to your life – and greater vitality to your body, mind, and spirit! Balancing your energies balances your body's chemistry, regulates your hormones, helps you feel better, and helps you think better. It has been called the self-care and development path of the future, but it empowers you now to adapt to the challenges of the 21st century and to thrive within them."

So, I started to practise Donna's energy balance methods daily, and began to incorporate them into my meditation classes too. Doing them first thing in the morning gives you a boost of energy and awakens your senses. For me, they help me to feel that connection to the Universe, feeling the life force energy flow through me.

I then began to look into Qigong (Qi meaning energy and Gong meaning work), which is an ancient Chinese healing practice that combines meditation, controlled breathing and gentle movement. It is an Asian form of yoga that has been around for thousands of years. The exercises follow the pathways of the energy meridians that run through the body and by tracing our energy field we allow the energy to flow. Benefits include; lower stress and anxiety, increased focus, and improved balance and flexibility. In Qigong, it's all about the focus, using the eyes to trace and focus on the movement, staying engaged in the body movements and being present. Qigong cultivates the energy and strength of nature into one's body to promote better mental, physical and spiritual health, which in essence is very similar to Donna's teachings; energy balance and having a connection to the chi (life force) energy, allowing it to flow as it should. These energy balance techniques are used for physical and mental healing and Qigong is also used in Tai Chi.

CHAPTER 6

Chakras

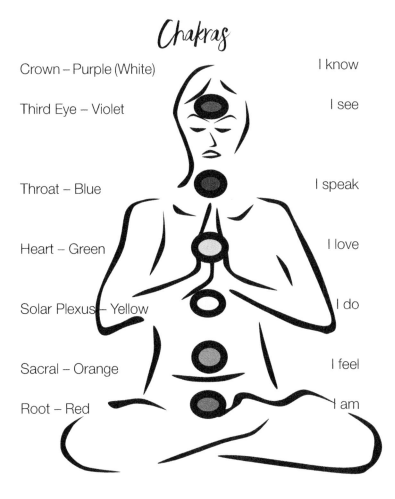

Crown – Purple (White)   I know

Third Eye – Violet   I see

Throat – Blue   I speak

Heart – Green   I love

Solar Plexus – Yellow   I do

Sacral – Orange   I feel

Root – Red   I am

Chakras also fall under the energy section of this book, but I have dedicated a new chapter to discuss them.

Let's take the word chakra, it's a Sanskrit word meaning 'wheel'. Chakras date back to ancient India, as early as 1500BC. Mentioning of chakras has been found in the first sacred texts of Hinduism. The chakra system has been an important concept in both Hinduism and Buddhism.

We all have an energy field around us; some people refer to it as your aura, which surrounds your physical body and extends out. These spinning wheels are vortexes of energy aligned along our spinal column within our energy field. They are the major focal points through which energy flows up and down the entire physical body. There are known to be around 114 chakras within our energy system, however there are seven major chakra dimensions that range from the base of your spine right up to the crown of your head.

Each chakra is responsible for regulating our physical functions as well as psychological like emotions and behaviour. Each chakra represents a certain part of your physical body, for example your organs; each chakra has its own vibrational frequency and its own colour. For example, our heart chakra is green, it has its own vibrational frequency, and it governs the heart and lungs as physical functions and also governs emotional functions such as feeling love and joy, how we build relationships, being compassionate and generous.

When you have imbalances in and around your chakras, it means that our Chi / Ki / Prana / Kundalini / life force energy (it's known as different names in different cultures) cannot flow through the energy system (chakras). Our life force energy flows through our energetic body by channels called 'nadis', which help the energy to flow and run like pathways between the chakras. If any of your chakras becomes blocked, underactive or overactive, you can become off balance physically, emotionally, mentally and/or spiritually, which then can have an impact on your health, emotional or behavioural states. These blockages of energy will manifest into symptoms of discomfort in these areas and can lead to negative aspects, such as ill health, poor mental health, pain, anxiety, stress, feeling exhausted and being unbalanced in the physical body. See from page 59 the negative and positive aspects of each chakra. Most of us have blocks in our chakra energy centres, which can then become symptoms in the physical body. As mentioned earlier, chakras can fluctuate daily depending on what is going on in your life. If you are able to elevate lower chakra energies and/or keep higher energies from sinking to a lower level, you are living a balanced and complete life. Aligning all seven chakras will help you to reach your fullest potential, taking back your power, living beyond the level of survival, beyond your social and physical aspect of living, stepping into the highest aspect of yourself so you can activate your energetic potential. When the chakras are all aligned, we are in balance with our life force energy and things go well for us in our everyday life, we are at peace, at one with ourselves, feeling love and having harmonious balance.

So, come on Sheryl, you ask, how do we do this? Well, the most common method to balance chakras is energy healing, which can include:

- Crystal healing
- Conscious breathing
- Chakra meditation
- Reiki
- Yoga
- Tai Chi

I am a crystal healer and, as part of my healing sessions with clients, I work on the seven chakra energy centres to balance these with crystals and energy work. I direct and focus energy through clear quartz crystals to balance the energy around each chakra centre. The crystals are cleansed and charged prior to use and are laid on the chakra centres, each crystal holding a vibrational frequency that matches that of the chakra. As the chakra absorbs the crystal's vibrations, the balance is restored. I also enjoy doing chakra balance meditation, which I perform during crystal healing sessions and as a standalone meditation that I practise on myself and in meditation classes and workshops.

Your chakras can fluctuate depending on how you are each day/ week/month and depending on what challenges you are going through in your life. So, keeping these in balance frequently can help to improve so much in your life in relation to you mentally, physically, emotionally and spiritually.

If you have a think about these physical and emotional aspects and see if you can relate to any, this will give an indication of which of your chakras need to be balanced.

The Seven Chakras, their meanings and aspects

THE ROOT CHAKRA (Muladhara) – The Colour Red

In order to balance your chakra system, you must first work on your root chakra, before you move through your other chakras. Getting the root chakra balanced so you have a steady foundation, you are feeling steady like the roots of a tree grounding you to Earth. A lack of 'roots' and not having a strong foundation can compromise all the other chakras, affecting the well-being of the entire body, mind and spirit. Only when we feel that we have our most essential needs met, can we then focus on growing and working on other areas (represented by the other chakra energy centres), being creative, having motivation and passion, feeling confident and leading us to be able to then form healthy relationships. The root chakra is known as 'the root of all things', associated with security, having a sense of stability in your life, feeling safe, being able to stand on your own two feet, being able to survive in the world and having basic human needs met; food, water, warmth, shelter, finances and having basic instincts that help us survive in life. We can't function in other areas when we don't have our basic needs met.

Your root chakra helps you to feel connected to Earth, so we are anchored physically in our bodies, being grounded and in control. Day-to-day feelings of trust, belonging and being present.

Physically it conducts energy to our hips, legs and feet and kidneys and stimulates the fight or flight function.

Positives / balanced aspects:

- You're present and feel rooted
- You have stability in life, feel secure, stable and at ease
- Your basic needs in life are being met
- You feel connection, have a connection to the Earth, you feel safe
- You're in touch with your body and feel at ease with your body
- You're nurturing
- You can trust others
- You are self-sufficient and responsible
- You feel supported
- You're in tune and like to be with nature

Negative / unbalanced aspects:

- Feeling insecure, depressed, unstable, disconnected from the present, powerless
- Being excessively negative
- It can lead to hoarding, greed, stealing
- Having a fear of the future and the inability to survive
- Feeling restless, unmotivated and feeling like you don't belong
- Fear of basic needs being unmet
- Under or overreacting
- Issues with organs around the root chakra; the rectum, including constipation, digestive issues, sciatica, lower back pain, anaemia

  – The root chakra can be balanced by saying and visualising the phrase "I am".
  – Take your awareness into your root chakra, visualise the colour red, a bright ruby red light that shines around your root chakra and, as you breathe, the light becomes brighter with each breath you take.
  – The root chakra chant is "Lam"; you can repeat this chant mantra to help balance the root chakra.

Affirmations to use:

- I am centred and grounded
- I belong, I am here, I feel safe
- I feel my connection to the Earth

- I am supported and protected
- I am accepted
- I trust and love my life
- I am financially free and secure

Grounding Techniques

When we feel disconnected, ungrounded, uneasy, restless, flighty, a bit lost, not centred, we can practise guided grounded meditation, which allows you to focus your mind on the present and learn to feel more balanced and aware. Grounding yourself can help you feel calm, peaceful and centred, having a connection, connect to Earth and back to centred awareness. Being grounded can mean two things: being fully present in your body and/or feeling connected to the Earth.

Grounding techniques can be used to help us feel rooted in our bodies; this will also help us control our anxiety and feeling out of balance, as we take our attention away from the negative thoughts and feelings and refocus to the present moment. Grounding is also called 'Earthing', which is a therapeutic technique where you ground or electrically reconnect yourself to the Earth. Doing things such as walking barefoot in nature, digging your toes into the grass, mud or sand and feeling the ground underneath you, bringing your awareness to it, feeling the soil or the grains of sand on your feet, feeling your connectedness. As you stand with your feet hip width apart, bring your focus to your breath and take a few deep cleansing breaths in and out. Then place your hands over your root chakra and imagine in your mind roots that grow out from the soles of your feet, as you take them right down deep into the Earth. You could say the affirmations as you ground your energy. Now imagine connecting to the Earth's energy, you can imagine it as the colour red. As you bring the red energy back up through those roots and into the soles of your feet, allow the energy to flow up through your legs and up into your root chakra. See your root chakra glowing with this bright red energy. Notice with each breath how relaxed you feel. Feel yourself grounding and feeling balanced, bringing you back to centred awareness. Grounding allows the physical connection between the electrical frequencies of the human body with Earth's electrical frequencies as they are exchanged. This can help us experience peace and inner stability, even when things around us feel chaotic or out of control.

You can also be grounded in the moment, such as when you feel the warmth of the sun on your skin or listen to the ocean waves as they lap up on the shore, as you smell the ocean. It's why many people are drawn to oceans and rivers. I love visiting the beach, looking out to the sea and watching the waves lap up towards the shore; it brings a sense of perspective to me, as my thoughts dissipate into a calm state and, in that moment, I feel totally grounded.

THE SACRAL CHAKRA (Svadhisthana) – The Colour Orange

The sacral chakra has received the nicknames 'the sex chakra', 'the social chakra' and 'the creation chakra'. The centre of your pleasure and passion, both sensually and creatively. This chakra governs reproductive systems, your sexuality, relationships, emotions, creativity and sense of adventure. It's also associated with your sexuality, your desires and pleasure, what you want in life.

When I say your emotions, it's where your emotions and your anxiety lies; when you get that anxious tummy, you can feel the imbalance in your sacral chakra. How we relate to emotions of ourselves and others.

Balancing your sacral chakra brings you motivation for success, following your passions and can help you manifest your ideas into fruition. It is the chakra of creativity. Now when I say creative, you sometimes think of arts and crafts, but it's not just being creative in an art and crafts sense, it can be being creative and finding enjoyment in something you're good at; computers, sport, cooking, whatever it is, bringing those creative ideas into existence. Try a new hobby or pursue a new idea or project that you have been meaning to do, follow your ideas, or you could try being crafty and make a gift for someone.

When this chakra is balanced you will feel alive, sensual,

desired and enjoyment, you will feel in touch with your emotions and trusting towards others. You'll feel motivated to achieve.

Positive / balanced aspects:

- Creative energy turning it into physical things (manifestation)
- Positive self-esteem
- Desire, pleasure / sensual
- Good fertility
- Enjoyment – seeking pleasure, having fun
- Sensuality
- Emotional balance
- Feel wanted and nurtured in relationships

Negative / unbalanced aspects:

- Issues with the reproductive system, including menstrual, urinary infections and lower back pain, issues with the bladder, kidneys, or adrenal glands can also arise (this is not to suggest these symptoms aren't from something else and nothing in here can replace a doctor's advice).
- A significant increase or decrease in sexual interest
- Becoming withdrawn, tense, insecure, needy, manipulative, controlling
- Having anxiety, worry, fear
- Feeling abandoned, left out

- Competitiveness
- Not caring for your body, feeling uncomfortable in your body
- Having difficulty pursuing creative endeavours

Try doing some physical exercises like hip circles to help bring energy and circulation to the sacral chakra.

- The mantra is, "I feel"
- Take your awareness into your sacral chakra, visualise the colour orange, a bright orange light that shines around your sacral chakra and, as you breathe, the light becomes brighter with each breath you take
- The chant is "Vam"

Affirmations to use:

- I am grateful for the body that supports and empowers me
- I let this orange light rebalance my emotions, my worries and anxieties
- I am thankful and joyful to be me
- I accept, embrace and celebrate my body
- I feel motivated for success
- I open myself up for creativity and passion to flow through me
- I allow my ideas to manifest and come into fruition

THE SOLAR PLEXUS (Manipura) – The Colour Yellow

Manipura in Sanskrit translates to 'city of jewels'.

The solar plexus is a vibrant energy centre, it is associated with your power, respect for yourself, self-confidence, self-esteem, your identity – how you see yourself, your image. Your freedom of choice, feeling happy and energised, being in control and having a zest for life. It is where your insecurities form, manipulation of others and how you set your boundaries with others.

Positives / balanced aspects:

- Strong sense of identity, positive self-image
- Strength of will
- Sense of purpose
- Feeling confidence (without being arrogant)
- Courageous
- Have feelings of achievement

Negative / unbalanced aspects:

- The need to dominate others
- Being judgemental and criticising others
- Aggressive, blaming others, irresponsible and being defensive
- Feeling like the world is against you
- Low self-esteem and confidence

- Nervous, like having a nervous tummy and anger turned inwards
- Physical issues can include gastric or digestion issues like stomach pain, nausea, a loss of appetite. More serious conditions like diabetes, hypoglycaemia and even eating disorders

  – The mantra is "I do" or "I can"
  – Take your awareness into your solar plexus chakra, visualise the colour yellow, a bright sunshine yellow light that shines around your solar plexus and, as you breathe, the light becomes brighter with each breath you take.
  – The chant is "Ram"

Affirmations to use:

- I am enough
- I have purpose, I am motivated to pursue my purpose
- I am confident
- Today I feel confident
- I can achieve anything I set my mind to
- I know who I am and I live true to myself
- I am strong, capable, and powerful
- I have the courage to create positive change in my life
- I am beautiful
- I am *more* than enough

THE HEART CHAKRA (Anahata) – The Colour Green

The heart chakra is the centre chakra of the chakra system, with three lower chakras and three upper chakras. It is the centre for compassion, empathy, love and forgiveness. Having a sense of trust, being fearless, finding peace, feeling generosity and gratitude, having healthy boundaries and relationships with others, and love for yourself.

When the heart chakra is balanced, you will feel more friendly and outgoing, you will be able to connect easily with others. You will be able to feel love and give and receive love with ease, you will experience healthy relationships with others and with yourself. It governs the thymus to bring strong immunity.

The heart chakra isn't pink or red, it's green like nature, like the Earth. A big green heart chakra planet, our planet of unconditional love.

Positives / balanced aspects:

- Unconditional love
- Peace
- Compassion
- Self-acceptance
- Healthy relationships
- Generosity

- Acceptance
- Openness
- Loving
- Good will

Negative / unbalanced aspects:

- Possessiveness
- Broken-hearted, unhappy, lonely, insecure
- Easily hurt, unable to receive and accept love
- Being distant from others and putting up barriers
- Shut down emotionally, or hold onto resentment or bitterness
- Jealousy
- Relationship issues / trust issues
- Lacking empathy
- Heart and circulatory problems, lung problems

  – The mantra is "I love"
  – Take your awareness into your heart chakra, visualise the colour green, a bright emerald green light that shines around your heart chakra and, as you breathe, the light becomes brighter with each breath you take.
  – The chant is "Yam"

Deep breathing can bring peace and calm to the heart and remove stuck or negative energy from the heart chakra. Engage in activities that spark love, passion and joy. Express your gratitude, feel the joy. Love yourself, feel proud of yourself.

Affirmations to use:

- I am worthy and deserving of love
- I am open to giving and receiving love
- I live with gratitude and generosity
- I am a loving being
- I have healthy and strong relationships, with others and myself
- I forgive myself and others

THE THROAT CHAKRA (Vishuddha) – The Colour Blue

The fifth, sixth and seventh chakras are the most spiritual of the seven.

The throat is associated with communication and self-expression, speaking your truth and finding your voice, expressing yourself. When this chakra is balanced it helps to set us free from the fear of judgement or need for approval from others.

This chakra helps us to embrace our originality and unique individual experiences in the world; you will feel you are able to voice your truth, speak with others with ease and improve your communication. You will be able to balance your speaking and listening, having effective communication skills. When your throat chakra is in balance, you may want to express yourself by making noise with your breath, hum or sing or express yourself through writing.

It also works closely with the sacral chakra; where the sacral chakra governs creativity, it is the throat chakra that allows the individual to *express* those creative ideas, rather than not following your passions for fear of other people's opinions.

Positives / balanced aspects:

- Clear communication
- Freedom of expression
- Truthful
- Outspoken

Negative / unbalanced aspects:

- Excessive talking, gossiping, talking over others, cursing
- Dominating conversations, complaining excessively, speaking aggressively or without thinking, not allowing others to express themselves, or needing to always be right.
- Inability to listen
- Fear of speaking out or holding things from people
- Physical ailments like laryngitis, sore throats, tension and pain in the neck, shoulders, or jaw, difficulties within the thyroid, lymph system, or pituitary gland, and problems with the teeth, gums, nose, ears, lower sinuses could arise

if the throat chakra is blocked (again I'm not a doctor and cannot replace one, these are just possibilities).

- Feeling shy, insecure, or socially anxious around others
- Choosing not to speak, or being unable to express oneself

  – Throat chakra mantra is "I speak"
  – Take your awareness into your throat chakra, visualise the colour blue, see this bright blue light melting tension from around the throat area and, as you breathe, the light becomes brighter with each breath you take
  – Chant is "Ham"

Affirmations to use:

- I live and speak my truth
- I allow myself to have a voice
- My voice is unique and valuable
- I freely and honestly use my voice to express myself
- I communicate clearly to others
- I know when to speak and I know when to listen
- I advocate for myself, and I stand up for what I believe

THE THIRD EYE CHAKRA (Ajna) – The Colour Violet

The Third Eye Chakra can be known as 'the seat of

intuition'. This chakra is your inner vision, your insight, your clarity of thoughts, where you can see things from a higher perspective, where you are in touch with the 'sixth sense' and your intuition. Helping you to further your connection to your spiritual self, gaining psychic awareness and the chakra to use to help develop spiritually. If you are working to improve your clairvoyant skills, you will work more on your third eye and crown chakras to communicate with spirit and enhance your psychic abilities.

As the most perceptive part of the human body and spirit, it governs self-awareness, higher wisdom, visualisation, clarity, imagination and creative dreaming.

It governs the pituitary, which influences metabolism, growth and hormones.

Positives / balanced aspects:

- In tune with psychic perception and visions beyond the physical realm
- Accurate interpretation
- In tune with your intuition, feeling clear guidance
- Good imagination
- Clear vision

Negative / unbalanced aspects:

- Nightmares / sleep disturbance
- Delusions

- Not in tune with your intuition, can't feel guidance
- Hallucinations
- Difficulty concentrating
- Poor memory
- Self-doubt, worry, overthinking, close-mindedness, feeling lost, or relying on others for validation and permission.
- Physical signs like tension in the brow area, headaches, eye strain, blurred vision, sinus issues, hearing problems, or dizziness.

  – The mantra is "I see"
  – Take your awareness into your third eye chakra, visualise the colour violet, a bright violet light harmonising your third eye chakra and, as you breathe, the light becomes brighter with each breath you take
  – The chant is "Aum"

Affirmations to use:

- I honour and trust my intuition
- I see and I know
- Everything is unfolding as it should
- I am connected to the Universe
- I have clarity and peace of mind
- I am receiving and I am trusting

THE CROWN CHAKRA (Sahasrara) – The Colour Purple (or White)

And we now come to the last energy centre of our seven-chakra system, The Crown Chakra, also known as 'the bridge to the cosmos'. It is the most spiritual in nature of all seven chakras.

The crown chakra is said to be the centre of our consciousness and the connection to the spirt realm and the Universe. It connects the mind, body and spirit as one. When balanced, you will feel enlightenment, feel the wisdom, feel the universal consciousness and connection to higher guidance. It governs interaction and communication with the Universe, knowing we are all one and all connected.

When your crown is balanced, you will feel your soul's purpose, you feel enlightened knowing that we are all connected and everything is love. It governs the pineal, which produces melatonin and regulates our body clock.

Positives / balanced aspects:

- Wisdom
- Knowledge
- Consciousness
- Bliss / oneness
- Spiritual connection

- Gratitude
- Understanding of your spirituality and place in the world
- Universal love

Negative / unbalanced aspects:

- Difficulty meditating
- Difficulty feeling connected, spiritual disinterest
- Not feeling connected to one's purpose
- Boredom
- Confusion
- Scepticism
- Limiting beliefs / judgemental / narrow-minded
- Depression
- Apathy
- Brain fog / issues learning

    – The mantra is "I know"
    – Take your awareness to the crown of your head, the crown chakra hovers a few inches from the top of your head, visualise the colour purple or white, as it shines around your crown chakra and, as you breathe, the light becomes brighter with each breath you take. Let the light filter down through your entire body, all the way into the soles of your feet
    – The chant is "Om"

Affirmations to use:

- I am connected to the Universe and to everything around me
- I am guided by something greater than myself
- I have access to wisdom and peace
- I honour my spirit and the divine within me

★★★

There are also other ways of working on your chakra energy centres, one of which is colour therapy. By wearing colours to represent our chakras, this can also be a reminder to give ourselves some time to think about the chakra. In your mind, take your awareness to the chakra and see the colour, feel it becoming balanced. For example, if you want to feel more confident, wear something yellow to coincide with your solar plexus. Think about your confidence, say an affirmation "today I feel confident, I can achieve anything I want" and take your attention down to your solar plexus; you could put your hand over it or do a clockwise motion to help balance the energy around the chakra. You could also light a candle of the colour or eat something of that colour. Surround yourself with the colour and spend some time balancing your chakra.

You can look at dancing to help balance your chakras, by shifting your energy to the chakra; for example for your root chakra, sway your hips, stomp on the ground, and as you bring your mind to the chakra, focus on it and intentionally think of balancing the energy around it. You can find out more by looking up chakra dancing online.

Balancing your chakras comes with some physical effort too. So now you know the traits of the chakras, try and remember these when you're talking to people, when you're going about your daily life. For example, if your heart chakra is out of alignment and you are trying to balance this using the colour green, doing meditation on the heart chakra, then you should also be conscious of how you are building your relationships with people (partners, colleagues, friends, family too), being compassionate, generous, kind and understanding. Work on each energy centre starting from the root up to the crown, using crystals, colour and energy healing, allowing you to feel in harmony and balance.

CHAPTER 7

Spirit Guides and Angels

What are spirit guides and angels? Well, everyone has spirit guides and angels, even if you're not consciously aware of them.

The word angel means messenger. I usually refer to spirit guides and angels in the same way, however I believe spirit guides are our personal guides, whereas angels are there for everyone and can be called when needed.

Spirit guides to me are our spiritual consciousness family, not particularly the family we have or have had here on Earth, but our 'other' family, our originating family. They are there to help direct us through life when we call upon them, helping us to see love and guide us to our best potential. They assist us through our human form. We often don't think about connecting with our guides, our busy lives rush by us and we seek answers from within ourselves instead, as we go on through life in our human form. It would be amazing if everyone knew how to connect with their guides, how to seek this guidance and loving energy, communicating for assistance in the physical realm. If we quieten our mind, we can communicate with them.

People do use spirit guides unconsciously without knowing or believing, for example, when people say a prayer, they are asking higher powers for guidance, which can also be known as spirit guides.

Prayer can be seen as religious, but you don't have to be religious to pray. Prayers can sometimes be associated with religion or that you must only pray to your God. We know from anthropological studies that prayer is one of humankind's oldest activities. People of all cultures pray in many forms and styles. I hear people say prayers consciously, "I pray I find love," and people will ask unconsciously, "Please someone show me the way." You will hear of people who are atheist who will use prayer in their time of need if something bad is occurring, "I know I don't believe in God, but if there is someone out there, please help me." We don't necessarily have to pray to our Lord or God. People tend to pray to ask for higher guidance or forgiveness, this is where our spirit guides can also help us.

Prayer is essentially a communication by word or thought, spoken out loud or said silently in the mind, towards God/source energy/higher power. In Christianity, we are told Jesus taught people to say the Lord's Prayer. The

Catholic Church highlights four basic elements of prayer in Christian religion:

1. Prayer of Adoration/Blessing,
2. Prayer of Contrition/Repentance,
3. Prayer of Thanksgiving/Gratitude,
4. Prayer of Supplication/Petition/Intercession.

There are different types of praying in my opinion:

1. Praying for something to happen,
2. Praying for guidance, please show me the way,
3. Forgiveness,
4. Gratitude, being thankful.

So, as you can see, there are lots of similarities in the way I see prayer to the way the Catholic Church sees prayer, and also who we pray to, the 'higher power', whether that be universal energy, spirit guides or a God.

So how can spirit guides help us? Spirit guides are with us all the time, whenever you need them, all you have to do is open your mind and talk to them, whether that be out loud or in your mind. So, you may feel silly at first talking to something you can't see, but if you open yourself up to the possibility of a response, you can hear if you quieten your mind and listen. Remember the four clairs I mentioned earlier; clairvoyant, clairaudience, clairsentient and claircognizance, these are the pathways to communicating with your spirit guides. Try asking a question, perhaps for some guidance on where you need to go next, or what course of action you need to take, or to help with finance, or heal a relationship, bring you confidence, whatever you need help with. Just remember to be specific with your questions, perhaps write them down first so you have a clear intention you can ask about, then quieten your mind, do some meditation breaths and wait for the guidance to come. Sometimes you hear words being spoken, or you may feel a presence and sometimes people can see their guides in their mind's eye. I always say it's important to follow the guidance you receive, but again sometimes it's hard to differentiate between your own thoughts and spirit guides, which is why meditation can really help with deepening the connection. Connecting with your spirit guides can be magical, and once you allow that relationship you can receive clear guidance to help you with aspects of your life, whenever you need it. Knowing there is a presence there supporting you can help you to feel calmer, safer and comforted living in our physical world, being able to interact with the non-physical, just knowing they are around to help guide us into alignment for our highest good. Always thank your guides for their help and support; appreciation and gratitude are key.

Some mediums will use the assistance from spirit guides to convey messages from the spirit world from passed souls to us in the physical dimension. You can book one-to-one sessions with a medium to have a personal reading where they will channel through messages from your loved ones who have passed. You can also visit a Spiritual Church. I have been to a number of services where I have found it to be a very relaxing experience. A service tends to take place first, occasionally the congregation will sing songs, and then a medium will get up to do the readings and give messages from spirit to the audience. I have never been picked to receive a message this way, but others I know have and have found it very comforting.

People do say that they have one main spirit guide, but it is known for people to have several spirit guides. I do believe this and have practised meditation to help strengthen this connection. Each time I do it, I am taken to one guide, a female of old age, very wise and she has long, white hair. This image of my spirit guide I see during a lot of my meditations. I'm going to admit that writing this book, when I read back, I think wow, did I write that? I use my guides for direction and sometimes once I begin writing the words just flow as if my guides are writing through me, the guidance and knowledge just comes to me, it's kind of cool! And I welcome you to try it out! Quieten your mind, do some meditation and connect with your guides, then grab a pen and paper and begin to write, you'll be amazed at what comes through you.

There are lots of meditation practices out there to help you deepen your connection and speak with your guides. Also, working on your Third Eye Chakra can help with connecting. I offer meditation sessions in a group and on a one-to-one basis to help strengthen the Third Eye Chakra and to work on connectivity to our guides/angels/higher realms. If you haven't tried it before, I suggest you give it a go, your guides are there to support you whenever you need it.

Angel oracle cards are another great way to help with connection to your guides and to give you guidance on what you need right now. Angel cards are an alternative to tarot cards, with helpful guidance and encouragement, with different pictures allowing you to interpret free-flowing guidance, rather than tarot, which are more structured and have common meanings. Everyone can seek guidance from their guides, you don't have to have some form of mystical power, however, some people are more in tune with tapping into the connection than others, and for some it takes a period of time to develop the ability. Each oracle card has a message and illustration from an archangel. When I work with these cards, I firstly find a quiet space and do some meditative breaths and connect to my guides and angels, and if I'm giving a reading to a client I also connect to theirs too. If I'm doing my own then I shuffle the cards (if I'm working with a client they will do this as their energy has an impact on the cards) and then ask a question, this could be for direction around a specific area of my or their life. Most popular choices tend to be around relationships, careers or a particular situation going on at that time. I then choose, or have my client choose, a card or two that I'm/they are drawn to. Occasionally a card will fall out of the deck as they are shuffled, and I know this is the card I need to read and observe. I look at the advice the card has to offer, not just from the text on the card, but from its illustration and any guidance that channels to me from the higher powers (my spirit guides and angels). The advice reflects on what is going on in your life and gives direction; sometimes it may not be the advice you wanted to hear, but always trust it, always!

There are several types of oracle cards on the market, from angels to mermaids, from positive affirmations to light workers. I suggest you have a look at what you're drawn towards and work with the cards when you receive them first before offering readings to others.

You can also use crystals to help with your readings, helping to deepen your connection. Have crystals laid out or in a grid form around the cards and holding or wearing crystals to help with the vibrational energy and connectivity.

Once you start working with your angels and guides, you will start to notice guidance, sometimes when you're not even looking! Seeing what are called 'angel numbers' that are a sequence of numbers, 111, 222, 333, 444, is quite common when working with angels and guides. I see these numbers frequently now and each time I let out a smile or sometimes a gasp as I know my angels are around me, showing me the way, confirming my life choices. Seeing these numbers means you are on the right track, like your angels are giving you a nudge to say, "We hear you, all is OK, you're on the right track." You can look up specific meanings for each number sequence, but I just like to know they are around me when I see these number patterns.

CHAPTER 8

Crystals

One day you'll find a nice shiny crystal, next thing you know you've got a collection of fifty-two different crystal types, five boxes of incense, sage sticks, tarot and angel cards, harem pants, a cauldron and magic wand! Yup that's pretty much how it started for me! Now where oh where do I start telling you about these beautiful little gems? Let me start at the beginning with  energy. Remember, we are all energy and have different vibrational frequencies; we want to raise our vibrational frequencies to let good things flow to us (also remember the Law of Attraction, like attracts like). Crystals have high vibrational frequencies, so when we hold a crystal and it comes into your energy field, you vibrate at that higher frequency, and that in essence is how crystals help us to heal.

The word 'crystal' derives from the Ancient Greek word κρύσταλλος (krustallos), meaning ice rock crystal. Hundreds of years ago they believed they had dug up water that had frozen so deeply in the Earth's core that it would always remain solid and never defrost, which is what gave it the name 'ice rock'. This was, of course, discovered to be untrue, as it wasn't water that would never defrost, it was in fact clear quartz crystal that they had found. So yes, crystals are part of the Earth, nature's own beauty, Mother Earth providing us with these beautiful natural crystals that have taken hundreds of thousands to even millions of years to form and grow. They are mined from the Earth for us to use.

Now, this is the scientific part, and you'll have to bear with me because I am no gemmologist or scientist. In basic terminology, a crystal is a natural solid made from minerals, made up of a collection of atoms that are repeated in exactly the same arrangement over and over, which gives them their unique properties. These molecules give the crystal its vibrational energy as it has a stable energy frequency, with its perfect geometric pattern of molecules that doesn't change. It is these vibrations that when placed around our energy field helps to regulate our energy. The energy from them can bring balance and healing and remove stagnant (blocked) energy. Crystals have also been shown to hold both heat and electricity and science can show that quartz crystals increase frequency of light passed through them. The quartz crystal oscillates (vibrates back and forth) at a precise frequency: exactly 32,768 times each second. This is used in quartz watches, which gives the watch its accurate time using the vibrations.

Some crystals when mined are tumbled into tumble stones, shaped into crystal wands and other patterns or can be left in their raw natural states.

Many cultures use crystals for healing, even in ancient times. Greek soldiers would rub hematite over their bodies before battle to keep them safe and protected. Talismans and amulets have been uncovered from Egyptian tombs decorated with crystals. The golden sarcophagus of King Tutankhamun is made with Lapis Lazuli crystals, which was a highly prized crystal in Egypt. Ancient Egyptians used crystals for protection and health and to keep away evil spirits and even cosmetically by grinding them into powder for dyes, eye shadow and used in medical elixirs. A medical elixir is a crystal that is placed into a glass of water, so you are drinking that vibrational frequency, because subtle energies can be charged and stored in water quite efficiently. But please remember to do some research as not all crystals are OK to ingest!

Crystal healing is a natural healing method where crystals are used as tools to help with the flow of energy. Crystals can be placed on the chakra energy centres and areas on and around the body to release negative (blockages of) energy and assist the Chi energy to flow as it should.

To work with the chakra energy centres, place a corresponding coloured crystal onto the chakra energy centre. To find the energy centres you can use a pendulum, by holding it steady in one hand over the area of the chakra centre you will find the 'pull' of energy and notice the pendulum spinning when it hits the energy centre. If it's moving quite rapidly around in a circle you can tell the chakra is out of balance. Moving it up the centre of the body over each chakra can help to identify what state each energy centre is in. Try working with a pendulum to start understanding the energy field. You can also move the pendulum around a person's aura, which will help you to pick out any imbalances (stagnant blockages) of energy. You can then leave the crystals on for 30-60 minutes or perhaps do a chakra balance meditation to help draw the energy from the crystals to balance the energy centres and to help you focus on each one.

Us humans have a real fascination with crystals and even if you've never seen or used them before you are always drawn to certain ones. In my experience, children love crystals. Whenever I am at a fair with my crystal stall, children always come over fascinated with the array of crystals and I love it! Crystals can be used in a number of ways, but the first thing you need to do is to choose your crystal. My advice is to always go with your intuition, don't worry about what the crystal means, go with your own guidance. Pick what you are drawn to; usually when you look at lots of crystals a few will 'jump' out to you, these are the ones you need to pick and work with. Once you have your crystals you can then read up on what properties the crystal holds, and what the crystal is said to be good for, for example it may say it's good for bringing positive energy or grounding your energy or building your confidence. However, I always advise to try each one separately and see how your energy resonates with the energy of the crystal first, see how it makes you feel.

Work with one crystal for a week or so; hold it, put it in your pocket, or if you have no pockets, you could pop one in your bra! Meditate with it, talk to it, it's your little crystal of peace, see how you feel when you have that crystal around in your energy field. Now people say to me, "Oh yes, Sheryl, I have one in my bag, I carry it around." Well, that's great for your bag, your bag is getting loads of great vibrational energy! But it needs to be on your person for you to be receiving that good energy. Another great way to ensure you have your crystals on you is to wear crystal jewellery. I always wear my crystal necklaces and bracelets and know I have that frequency on me all day long.

Crystal healing is best done in a relaxing environment, with quiet meditation music. During my crystal healing sessions in my healing room, I create a calming space using incense, candles, essential oils and meditation music. Clients will lay down on the bed and I work with the energy field using my hands and crystals to direct and balance their energy. I also focus my energy into each chakra energy centre to help bring them to balance. I use quartz crystal to help facilitate this and numerous other crystals, which are placed around and on the body.

Meditation is another section I am going to be speaking about but let me tell you now, crystals help to intensify and deepen your meditation practice. See which ones work best for you, it's always trial and error. Place the crystal, ideally a palm stone (tumblestones are good too), in your hand and you can focus on the crystal or just have it there or around you while you're in your meditation practice, or place on your chakra energy centres to do a full chakra balance meditation.

You can place crystals around your home to balance the energy within your house. Amethyst is a great piece to have as it brings a positive energy to your home and has a high vibration. Selenite is a beautiful, calming crystal and has cleansing energy, which helps to cleanse the surrounding space, this includes your energy, your home's energy and anything surrounding it, so it's an ideal crystal to use to cleanse your other crystals.

It is also said that putting crystals in a grid pattern in all four corners of a room can help intensify the energy, using black crystals to ward off negative energies around your home. You can also use crystal grids to set up and direct an intention into it; for example, to find love, make a crystal grid of a mix of rose quartz and green crystals, using clear quartz to intensify the energy and put in your intention to the grid of it helping you to find love and healing, to help balance your heart centre to attract joy and love.

There are so many crystals out there with so many ways they can help you. As I said before, it's best to go on how that crystal makes you feel, don't get bogged down with their meanings. However, if you do want a crystal for a specific reason, then it's good to choose one that will help you for that purpose. I have listed below some good crystals to use along with their crystal properties.

Amethyst – A protection and cleansing crystal, with a high vibrational energy, it helps to protect your energy and bring positive/higher frequency energy to you. Amethyst can help to relieve stress and strain, tension, pain. Amethyst helps enhance spiritual awareness, opens your intuition and psychic abilities, use it on your Third Eye Chakra.

Aventurine (green) – Comforts, harmonises and balances the Heart Chakra, it can be used to help attract love and develop positive relationships. Green Aventurine has a soothing energy and is recommended for working through emotional issues. Ideal to use for soothing tempers bringing about calm and peace, especially within relationships.

Amazonite – Ideal to use for combatting stresses, healing traumas and soothing energies, and also used to help with overcoming loneliness. Called the 'Stone of Courage' and the 'Stone of Truth', Amazonite assists in communicating one's true thoughts and feelings without over-emotionalism.

Angelite – A high vibrational crystal that helps to harmonise the Throat Chakra along with helping to develop spiritual awareness within the Third Eye and Crown Chakras. It brings you serenity with its tranquil feel and nurturing, soothing blue colour. Angelite is said to help develop your spiritual awareness and can help with developing psychic abilities. With a peaceful energy that is calming and soothing, assisting with the connection to your angels, spirit guides and the higher realm and to help feel your angel's divine love.

Black Onyx and Agate – Powerful grounding and protection crystals, absorbs and transforms negative energy and helps to prevent the drain of personal energy. Helps to bring emotional and physical strength during difficult times. Wear or carry Onyx for protection and to help with fighting fears. Helping to ground your energy, feel presence and awareness and connection to Earth. Use on the Earth Star Chakra, a few inches under the feet.

Botswana Agate – Ideal crystal for emotional healing to rebalance your emotions. You can use it as a comfort crystal and can be beneficial in overcoming depression, and to help during a grieving process. An ideal crystal for sensitive children who are easily hurt by teasing or pressure.

Bloodstone – An excellent blood cleanser and a powerful healing stone. It is a good grounding and protection crystal. Bloodstone draws off negative environmental energy, helping to overcome influences such as geopathic or electromagnetic stress. It can help to bring vitality as it clears out negative energy. Bloodstone helps to activate inner strength, willpower and courage, helping to get the energy flowing in your mind, body and spirit. Use on the Heart Chakra.

Citrine – Helps to balance and energise the Solar Plexus, bringing you confidence, personal power and drive. Called The Merchant's Stone for its properties of increasing abundance, attracting wealth, prosperity, success and all things good.

Carnelian – Brings vitality and motivation, courage and confidence. Promotes positive life choices and motivates for success. Helps you to develop your creative side, follow through with your ideas and manifest your dreams. Use on the Sacral Chakra.

Clear Quartz – Known as the 'Master healer' it brings the body into balance and will amplify energy and thought, as well as the effect of other crystals. It absorbs, stores, releases and regulates energy. Clear Quartz draws off negative energy. It balances your physical, mental, emotional and spiritual energies. Clear Quartz can also help to enhance your psychic abilities. Use on the Crown Chakra.

Fluorite – Used for cleansing the mind, body and spirit of stress, anxiety and negative energies, it helps to remove impurities, bringing them to surface, and ensures balance and harmony. It is useful for spiritual development, connectivity to higher dimensions. It carries a calm, stable frequency that brings harmony. It enhances positive energy around you. Use on the Third Eye and Crown Chakra.

Howlite – A lovely calming crystal to use when needing to reduce anxiety, tension, anger and stress with a soothing energy. Helps to soothe emotions, slow an overactive mind and achieve a deep and restful sleep.

Lapis Lazuli – Helps to balance the energies around the Throat and Third Eye Chakra. Helps to activate the higher mind and enhances intellectual ability. Helps to retain information and assist in learning knowledge. Helps to strengthen communication with others, speaking out your truths and ideal when speaking to a group/public speaking.

Moonstone – A great feminine energy crystal used for new beginnings and manifesting. A crystal for inner growth and strength. It soothes emotional instability and stress, and stabilises the emotions, providing calmness. Moonstone enhances intuition, promotes inspiration, success and good fortune. It has a soothing influence and relaxing effect, which bring a sense of composure.

Red Aventurine – Helps to manifest ideas into fruition. Boosts vitality and mental alertness and amplifies the desire to take on life's challenges with determination and perseverance. It inspires creativity and sexuality, and renews excitement and confidence in bringing one's projects, goals and desires into reality. Use on the Sacral Chakra.

Red Jasper – A protective and grounding crystal. The colour red is associated with luck. Jasper can be used on the Root Chakra to balance the energy centre, helping you develop a more balanced attitude towards the physical world. Helps to ground to the Earth and find purpose.

Rose Quartz – A calming and reassuring crystal, excellent for use in trauma or crisis. It strengthens empathy, sensitivity, and is an excellent crystal to use for comforting grief. Rose Quartz can be used to help with sleep, bringing beautiful dreams as well as preventing nightmares for both adults and children. It can help to heal emotional wounds, fears and resentments. Brings a divine loving energy throughout the entire aura and strengthens loving relationships. You can incorporate this crystal with the Heart Chakra along with green crystals.

Selenite – A calming crystal that instils deep peace and relaxation. It is excellent for use during meditation or spiritual work with a high vibrational energy. It has a very soothing and calming presence. Selenite brings about purification, cleansing and positive energy. Placing selenite in a room brings this beautiful cleansing energy into the room and can help to cleanse your energy field and crystals too! Carry and meditate with selenite to also receive these benefits. Helps to balance the Crown Chakra and the Soul Star Chakra

Smoky Quartz – A powerful grounding and balancing crystal, releasing negative energies such as jealousy, fear and anger. Smoky Quartz is a grounding stone known for its ability to help you move on from painful memories of the past and letting go. It is said to be great for soothing pain, both emotional and physical.

Sodalite – A strong vibration crystal that helps to brings order and calmness to the mind, helping to reduce stress and tension. It is particularly helpful to help the development of psychic abilities and develop your intuition. This crystal may help you if you are doing public speaking and helps to strengthen your communication with others. It enhances self-esteem, self-acceptance and self-trust. Ideal to use around the Throat Chakra.

Tree Agate – A crystal for inner peace. It helps to calm nerves, bringing calming and centring energies. It is also a good crystal for grounding and helping you to connect on a deeper level to the Earth and with nature with its powerful healing vibrations. In Feng Shui, it brings the energy of nature into your space.

Tiger's Eye – A crystal that helps you to release fear and anxiety and aids harmony and balance. It helps you to take action, giving you courage, confidence and strength of will. This crystal is of benefit to those who are suffering from mental illness or with personality disorders. Keep Tiger's Eye as a stone of luck and good fortune. Wear or carry Tiger's Eye for increasing insight and perception in unfamiliar places or circumstances. Helping to manifest desires to reality. Use around the Sacral Chakra.

Unakite – A kind and compassionate crystal. Helping to develop, balance and nurture your emotional health. The emotional healing properties of Unakite are incredibly powerful because of the unique combination of pink feldspar and green epidote. Ideal crystal to use to help heal the Heart Chakra and help to balance love relationships. Unakite supports recovery from ill health. It is also believed to affect the reproductive system, healthy pregnancy and the growth of skin and hair.

Yellow Carnelian – A great uplifting, revitalising and motivational crystal, giving you a zest for life. It can help to increase willpower, concentration and confidence. Use Yellow Carnelian for the Solar Plexus Chakra to help you gain more confidence and positive self-esteem, seeing yourself in a positive image, as well as the ability to learn from your past mistakes, reinforces courage, confidence, happiness and prosperity into your life.

Zebra Agate – an efficient grounding stone and a powerful stimulant for artistic creativity. When doing spiritual work, this crystal keeps you connected to the Earth. Helps to clear energy blockages and emotional pain to bring about inner balance, relieving inner tension. With its mix of black and white, it connects polarities and opposites – spirit with matter, balancing the yin with yang. It balances the connection between Earth and sky, grounds you while elevating spiritual awareness.

Cleansing Crystals

Once you have your crystal, you must first look to cleanse it. As a crystal has been mined, then travelled long distances and brought into shops, it means several people could have held that crystal and their energies could affect the crystal's energy as the crystal stores energy. You want it to be cleansed as much as possible to have optimal healing effects for you. I have noted some ways you can cleanse your crystals on the following pages. My favourite is to use sage because you can use sage on all your crystals, your space and even your person! You can cleanse your whole house with sage to help get rid of any negative energies and bacteria in the air.

Natural methods such as using the elements of nature (fire, water, Earth and air) are very effective in cleansing crystals of negative energies. It is important that while you are cleansing your crystal you hold the intention in your mind of carrying away unwanted energies.

SMUDGING –

Burn the white sage smudge stick at the end until it starts to smoke, carefully pass the crystal through the smoke until you intuitively feel the crystal is cleansed. I like to watch the way the smoke forms around the crystal, which is when I know it's cleansed.

WATER –

Rinse the crystal through running water until you intuitively feel the crystal is cleansed. Do NOT use water on soft crystals such as angelate, calcite, howlite, aragonite, azurite, dolomite, malachite, selenite, sulphur. A usual rule to go by is if the crystal ends in 'ite' use an alternative cleansing method. Please research first as water can damage some crystals.

EARTH –

You can bury your crystal in the ground overnight; it is advisable to bury in a plant pot as you may lose your crystal (do not use potting soil as this is treated).

SEA –

Place your crystal in a mesh/organza type bag, rinse it in the ocean for several minutes, or soak in a glass full of salt water for several hours. Caution with this method as salt may damage the finish on some crystals and water may not be advisable to use on some crystals as stated before.

SUNLIGHT –

Place the crystal in sunlight (ideal place on a windowsill). CAUTION: crystals having been formed within the Earth devoid of any light, sunlight may be too harsh for some crystals and also may fade the colour if done regularly, but this is a quick/easy method.

MOONLIGHT –

Place the crystal under moonlight when it is a full moon overnight on a windowsill, helping to absorb and cleanse the crystal full of moon energy.

SOUND –

Use a bell, chime, tuning fork, singing bowl or tingshas. If you create a pure tone this will reset a crystal's vibration.

Step 1 – Choose your crystal.
Step 2 – Cleanse your crystal.
Step 3 – You are now ready to use your crystals, meditate with them, carry them on your person, place in your home or make a grid.

CHAPTER 9

Meditation

In our world today we have so much to deal with on a daily basis, from stresses at work, relationships with partners, family, friends, colleagues, trying to juggle family and work-life balance, needing to remember everything for the day ahead, thinking  about what to have for tea, remembering which bin it is I need to put out this week, what the children need for the day, for school, homework, clubs, getting them to school on time, have we eaten our five a day? I need to exercise, did I remember to renew the gas/electric/water/car/home insurance, did I pay that bill? Am I socialising enough? Did I wish X a happy birthday? Did I do that report for work? Am I doing enough for me? The list is pretty much endless as we continue to try to keep everything afloat! No wonder so many people are living hectic lives, leading to depression and anxiety and other mental health illness, our minds are continuously thinking about the past or the future.

When we are caught up in everything we have to do each day, our mind becomes 'boggled' and we can't think straight, do you ever say that? "I have so much going on I just can't think straight." Once you start meditating, enjoying the relaxation it brings, finding that inner peace, the balance, letting the crazy chattering monkey mind of thoughts settle down, you begin to understand when and why your body needs to just stop and meditate! You emerge from your meditation practice with more clarity, being able to think clearly and with more focus, enabling you to see your day clearer and be able to deal more effectively with anything that occurs throughout your day. Meditation has heaps of benefits and can help to greatly improve your life from your overall well-being to helping you have more focus and clarity of the mind, not to mention the array of health benefits; it strengthens the vagus nerve that helps to reduce stress and anxiety, can improve sleep, lower blood pressure, help to deal with pain, improve your self-image and outlook on life, being more aware and having an awareness of your self, your true self, how you deal with situations, bringing you clarity, a calmer mind, improving your attention span, self-control and awareness of triggers for addictive behaviors.

Our minds are constantly working and producing thoughts *all* the time, day in, day out, our thoughts constantly on the hamster wheel. We need to tame that crazy monkey mind of thoughts down to give our brain some time out; just like you would sit down and rest your body if it was aching, we are resting our minds to allow them to be in a state of peace, to access the true nature of awareness without the clutter of thought, allowing the experience of being in the present moment. Using meditation practice can help us to be mindful and get out of the continuous thought patterns, observing our thoughts, our emotions and feelings, noticing our anxiety and stress in an alternative perspective, without judgement, just being aware and noticing. For example, if you're meditating and become aware of feelings of stress, you begin to notice it in a way you may not have noticed before, you're aware of it, you can observe it, begin to see where in the body the stress affects you, perhaps noticing it in your stomach or your chest, you can breathe into it to allow the stress and these feelings to dissipate and make it less unpleasant, by observing it and shifting your perspective.

"Sheryl, I can't meditate, I've tried, I just can't shut off." Do you know how many people have said this to me? I can tell you, it's a lot! My response is, you can't *fail* to meditate. Meditation isn't about getting rid of *all* thoughts (which can be achieved if desired), however, it's more about stilling the mind and being able to use this practice of observing thoughts, emotions and feelings when they occur and having the ability to take our awareness back, shifting the focus back to the breath. We use the breath as it's always there with us wherever we are, we always have our breath, by focusing on the breath it allows our mind to stabilise, to free it so you can observe things in a non-reactive way. Meditation is a mindful technique, being aware of the present moment, not worrying about the past, what's happened during your day or worrying about what's going on in your life or worrying about what's to come, what you need to do, what you're having for tea, what you need to say to someone, events or situations that are upcoming. Nothing else matters during mindfulness meditation, all there is is the present moment; being in a more relaxed state, aware of your body, mind, thoughts, feelings, observing and being at peace in the present moment. This allows us to then connect to our true self. During meditation, you can connect with your inner self, the calm self, finding the true you, allowing outside distractions to fade away and turning our awareness inwards.

Even by closing your eyes for a few minutes, focusing on the breath, being in the present moment, being aware, observing any thoughts or feelings that arise, this is meditation. You don't *have* to sit for hours, although deepening your practice requires extended time frames. Meditation is a practice, it's like going to the gym, you don't expect a fit body and muscles on day one, so of course your mind won't stop thinking during your first meditation practice. It takes practice! The more you practise, the longer you will be able to be in a meditative state. Try ten minutes to start and gradually increase; before you know it, you will be doing half-hour meditation practices without realising!

The ego tries to avoid meditation. It always manages to convince you that doing something is always better than doing nothing. Committing yourself to regular meditation practice is the first victory over your ego. This was me and still is at times! I have always been a person who must be on the go, I struggled with sitting doing nothing, thinking I am wasting my time; the cleaning still needs to be done, I need to prep dinner, I still have my accounts to sort out, I should be out socialising. There lies the reason we *need* to meditate, it's not wasting your time, it's creating time. What I mean by this is when we are rushing about in our daily lives, we forget to breathe, we forget to be in the present moment. When we do meditate, we create more presence, being able to get on with our day with a clearer focused mindset, where you can then in return be more productive.

The present moment, that's all there is, the present. The past has been, the future is yet to come, being mindful is all about being in the present moment. Are you present right now? Are you reading these words and taking them in, or is your mind wandering and you have to reread sentences as your mind drifts. Being mindful is about being *aware*, having awareness of how you're feeling right now, how your body feels right now, what's occurring in your mind right now. If you're doing a task or even if you're eating, being present and aware of every movement of your task is being mindful. For example, how many times do you take a shower and not embrace the warmth of the water, feel it flowing over your hair and skin, how many of you let your minds wander to things you need to do today, things that have been in the past that resurface, and not fully being present? Taking a shower will never be the same again after reading this. Try it, be present, don't let your mind wander, feel every moment. How about when you put your make-up on or get dressed, where is your mind? Do you feel the brush strokes? Are you present? Do you feel your clothes, the material on your skin? Or do you rush putting them on and let your mind think about your day? When you eat do you enjoy each mouthful, do you taste your food, the textures? I know I haven't always been present when eating a takeaway, excited for the knock on the door, rushing to get the plates out, and spooning my food in like I've not had a meal for a week! Being mindful and present allows you to enjoy these experiences without the rush of life and thoughts around your mind.

We are always thinking about the future or the past, and rarely allow ourselves to live in the present. Try it, when you eat, when you walk, when you have a shower/bath, when you get ready, when you watch TV, when you're at the beach or having a stroll through nature. Let yourself be truly present.

There are various types of meditative practices out there: visualisation, guided, Zen, Christian and religious, mantra, walking, mindfulness, transcendental, chakra balance. My favourite is Zen breathing meditation, which allows us to have the time out our body and mind need, slowing down the thoughts and being in the true present moment. Even for just ten minutes a day this amazing practice can bring you so much. Basically, all you need to do is close your eyes, be in a seated, upright position (position is important to help facilitate diaphragmatic breathing), and focus on the breath; each time you observe a distraction or a thought pops up in your mind, allow it, witness it, and let it pass, taking your awareness back to the breath, accessing true awareness without clutter of thoughts. Continue to do this for at least ten minutes.

Meditation is the key concept for stilling the mind and you can practice it anywhere at anytime, jut allow it and enjoy the peace and stillness it brings you. As you drift into the unconscious state of mind, allow the body to rest, the mind to rest, to achieve inner peace. Where nothing else matters.

Meditation quietens conscious thought and can help open the doorway to spiritual awareness. Once you enhance your inner vision with deep meditation, connection can be made with your spirit guides and angels, it's the gateway to the unknown. Practising meditation can greatly help with your clairvoyant skills and practising mediumship, if you choose to go down that route.

Visualisation meditation is a great way to take you out of everyday life, letting the mind settle and going on a visually guided meditation journey. It could be anywhere, such as a relaxing place, a garden, beach, nature or visualising your negative energy being released or infusing positive energy to us.

Mantra meditation and transcendental meditation are similar practices, choosing a word or phrase to repeat silently in your mind or speak or chant out loud. This is done throughout the whole, or part, of your meditation. You don't have to use ancient words such as Sanskrit for mantra meditation, although some words have a good vibration to them when speaking out loud. You can choose a word or phrase that has a positive resonance with you: see Chapter 11 for Positive Affirmations that can be used as mantras during meditation. Mantras are used to focus the mind, connect to the heart and the divine within you. Buddhists say that it helps to keep the mind focused and receptive to the blessing of the present moment. My favourite mantra is Ong Namo Guru Dev Namo; it's a beautifully moving mantra, which contains the vibration of peace, prosperity and connection, helping you to centre yourself and tune into your own inner being, your true self, opening yourself up to receive guidance and wisdom from the divine. The mantra asks you to believe in your own internal guidance, seeking your own intuition and listening to your inner wisdom. Ong meaning the creative energy of the divine/the Universe, Namo meaning to bow to/greet you, Guru meaning teacher, the giver of wisdom bringing you from the darkness into the light, Dev meaning divine and Namo again meaning to greet you/bow to you.

My recommendation for meditation is to try a few different types out, there's not a one box fits all, some people prefer being guided, some prefer to sit in total silence, while others prefer visualisations to get them into that relaxed state. Remember not to get stressed with yourself if you can't 'shut off', as I said above, it's not about totally removing all thoughts, it's more about awareness, being present and letting the mind settle.

CHAPTER 10

Gratitude

"Your gratitude is magnetic, the more gratitude you have the more abundance you magnetise, it's the universal law."
~ Rhonda Byrne

I don't believe people realise how important gratitude is. Gratitude can help to turn us around, get us out of the negative, impatient frequency and can shift us quickly into a different, higher vibration. Gratitude and anxiety cannot exist at the same time.

We are always looking at the bad things that are happening in our lives, we are always moaning about things, sharing our problems with our friends. I have also noticed a huge increase of negativity on social media, it's swamped with people posting nasty hateful comments; even on positive posts you see people really being hateful towards other people. It really saddens me that this happens so much and it's rare that we actually talk about the things we are grateful for and the good things going on in our lives. It may feel daunting at first, as we aren't used to thinking and talking about things in life that are going well. But once you get into it, it really is easy because there are so many things right here right now that we can all be grateful for.

If you feel the love and appreciation of things around you, and you feel in your body the resistance melting away, it can shift your state into that higher vibration. I have also read that when you're practising gratitude, happy hormones (like endorphins, serotonin, oxytocin and dopamine) flood your brain, which invites in positive vibes that can help you, in turn, to have better relationships and can reduce stress levels. This can then lead to a joyful, positive life. So, what's stopping you from trying it?

I talk about gratitude all the time – during my meditation classes, during my workshops, during healing sessions, on my social media groups – because I know and understand the importance of it, how it can shift your energy and practising it every day can be an absolute life changer. I know because I practise it and I share my knowledge with my clients who have told me how beneficial it has been to them.

Now you may think, "Well, what can I be grateful for, Sheryl? I'm so down right now, I am depressed, nothing is going right for me, I can't be grateful for anything!" Well, let me tell you, it doesn't matter where you are in your life or what is going on around you, even if you feel you are rock bottom. Start by feeling your gratitude for everything you already have, and once you start, you will start to feel and see that change, feel the appreciation, the abundance, and watch the LOA do its thing.

> *"The moment you start acting like your life is a blessing, it starts feeling like one.*
>
> *Each of us is attracting in every moment of our lives. So, when you feel that the law of attraction isn't working for you because you don't have what you want, realize that the law is constantly responding to you."*
>
> ~ *Quote Law of Attraction*

Remember the LOA is working whether you are aware of it or not, what you give out, and are in energetic harmony with, you receive, so just think for a moment about what gratitude could do, if we appreciate what we have, really feel the appreciation, those waves are being sent out there for you to receive back. So, what can you be grateful for? Well, I shall share some of my gratitudes that you could try to help shift that mindset to positive thinking, that abundance that you can feel whenever you choose. And that is the joy of it, you can do this anytime, anywhere. Now I follow a few inspirational authors/teachers and I do like to follow their practices, the ones that resonate with me. Remember, this book is all about what resonates with you,

you don't have to do things as outlined, take everything with a pinch of salt, or hey, follow it by the letter, you can do whatever you choose as long as it feels good and works for you!

Things to be grateful for, adapt as you wish:

- My home, my garden because …
- My job because …
- All the money that I earn because …
- My car/transport because …
- My family (son, daughter, mother, father, partner/wife/ husband, whoever) because …
- My friends because …
- My pet because…
- My TV, Netflix, all the platforms available to me because …
- The food that I eat, the wide variety of choice that is available to me because …
- Being able to cook because …
- Having a shop at the end of the street because …
- Having fresh, clean water to drink in an instant because …
- Having electric, gas, central heating available to me at all times because …
- Having the internet because …
- My love for crystals because …

- The sun, the moon, the stars, the Earth, Mother Nature because …
- Flowers, trees, plants because…
- My couch because …
- My senses, my eyes to see, ears to hear, nose to smell, mouth to taste because …
- Having a GP surgery close by, the NHS because …
- Feelings of love, happiness, joyfulness because …
- Meditation because …
- Being able to sleep well at night because …
- Having a bed to sleep in and warm blankets because …

Honestly, once you start it's hard to stop! Some of these things aren't available to people and we must appreciate every single thing we have in our lives and think about why you are grateful for them, feel the happiness you create when you say them, and then at the end of each one say "thank you" three times to cement that blessing. Get yourself into a routine of doing your gratitudes every day; set a time of the day to focus on them, I do mine every night before bed and I spend ten minutes thinking about three things I am grateful for that day, really feeling the appreciation for what I have. Throughout my day, I now automatically start appreciating things; if I receive an order or booking, if I've had a nice meal, even just acknowledging that water is freely flowing from my taps for me to drink, appreciating my cup of coffee in the morning. Why not start writing a gratitude journal? If you turn to the end of this book, you will find some blank pages to begin your own gratitude diary. Make some notes each day for things you are grateful for and read over them during your day or before bed, which is ideal to help reinforce the gratitude and appreciation.

So, this is your challenge now, start doing some gratitudes every day and see how you get on.

CHAPTER 11

Positive Affirmations

A positive affirmation is a word or phrase used to reset your mind and allow our vibrational energy to rise to a higher state, allowing the vibration of the words to create the shift in our energy.

Choose a word or phrase that you can relate to or inspires you, or an affirmation for something that you want to achieve or become, which has a positive influence to encourage positive change in your life. These words or phrases can be used during meditation or can be used every day as a reminder to you to shift your mindset, to motivate you, to inspire you, to get you out of the negative spiral of thoughts. Like attracts like, therefore being in a more positive frame of mind helps good positive things to flow to us. If you become stuck in negative thought patterns, the tumbleweed effect can lead us on a downward spiral, attracting more negative occurrences into our lives. Positive affirmations help us to break that cycle and change our mindset and our vibrational energy, to lift our spirits and remember you can, you are good enough, you can achieve, you can be the best version of you.

If you practice regularly and incorporate affirmations into your everyday life, you will start to see the changes. It can help you feel more empathy, less aggression, feel more balance, calm, and even sleep better, making a difference to how you feel and how you view yourself and the world.

We can all create results in our life, visualising success, whatever you want can be achieved effortlessly. Set an affirmation for every time you do a task that it will be achieved effortlessly. "I can achieve anything I set my mind to effortlessly."

As you read through the affirmations below, let yourself feel the words, as you resonate with the phrases and notice any change in your inner self. As you say each one out loud or in your mind, take a breath in and exhale out.

- Today is a good day, today really is a good day, today I choose to feel good
- I will be grateful for every moment of today
- I have all I need to make today a good day
- I choose to let go of the old and allow a new path before me for a positive future
- Today my new life begins
- I allow myself to feel peace, I know my breath brings me back to peace

- I feel motivated and inspired; motivated for positive change, inspired to make positive changes
- I am grateful for the people I have in my life, I appreciate the people I have in my life
- Every day in every way, I am getting stronger
- I allow myself to be who I am without judgment
- I am enough, I am worthy, I am more than enough
- Everything I need is within me
- I can achieve anything I set my mind to
- I have strength, I have confidence
- I listen to my intuition and trust my inner guide
- I always do my best and it's enough for me to know that
- I'm doing well and it's getting better
- I am full of energy and optimism for my day ahead
- I am ready to find joy in everything I do
- I can overcome negative thoughts and situations. I can choose positive thoughts
- I release my negative thoughts, about myself and around situations in my life, I replace them with positive thoughts – I am enough, I am beautiful, my life is good
- I am committed to having 'me time' today
- I embrace my best self today
- I have abundant energy, vitality and well-being
- I love to smile, I can smile today (smile now)
- My body is healthy, my mind is healthy, I am ready to start the day
- What I focus upon causes an attraction of things that match it

- Whatever I want can flow to me
- Things are always working out for me
- I am open to the possibilities of the Universe
- Today is going to be a great day, today is a good day, this is the start of a brand new day, I look forward to today and everything that welcomes me
- I raise my vibration with my positive mind, I raise my vibration with my positive feelings

CHAPTER 12

Moon Rituals

The moon has eight cycles/phases, going from full moon, into waxing gibbous, to frist quarter, waxing crescent, new moon, waning crescent, third quarter, waning gibbons and back to full moon. We can use the moon as a guide to manifest the life we want; knowing which phase she is in can help us to set our intentions and release what we no longer need. Some people think it sounds a bit 'woo-woo', but when you look into our history, we only had the moon, sun, stars and planets to go by. Our ancestors planted, hunted, fished and travelled by the seasons and cycles of the moon, and some still do. For example, farmers still plant by the moon phases, moisture is pulled toward the top layer of the soil and improves germination. In ancient times, the moon was observed to change over a twenty-nine-day period that coincided with a woman's reproductive cycle. It is said that the moon is feminine and has a feminine energy. People have worked with the moon cycles for centuries to manifest their dreams. In our modern-day times, we have such a disconnection from this, and learning to meditate, follow moon cycles, manifest and release with the moon phases can be life changing! Feeling in alignment with the planets helps us to feel grounded and brings feelings of peace. Learning when to start life events, projects and opportunities and when to let go of what we no longer need to hold onto. It's also great to follow as it gives us an opportunity and reminder to check in with ourselves.

You can also delve deeper, should you choose, and look into your horoscope using your birth date and time as a guide to manifest and set intentions around different aspects of your life, depending on which sign of the zodiac the moon is in.

> *"Manifesting with the moon's cycles as a cosmic timer dramatically boosts our chances of becoming accomplished conscious creators and deliberate manifestors."*
>
> ~ *Yasmin Boland*

Full Moon

A full moon occurs towards the end of each monthly lunar cycle. Our own emotions and thoughts tend to flow in sync with the moon and can become heightened towards and during the full moon cycle. Some days you may find yourself full of energy and some days feeling drained and down; just as the phases of the moon affect the seas with its gravitational pull, generating tidal forces where the water is pulled towards the direction of the moon, they can also affect our emotions and we feel the flowing surges of energy through us; remember, we too are made of 70% water! When the moon is full, it is in perfect alignment with the sun and is closest to the Earth, so we feel its energy more so. Many cultures believe that the full moon each month cleanses all that it touches. At each full moon, we can allow ourselves to become cleansed with its energy, it's a time to slow down and reflect on the past month and is said to be a time when the seeds (manifestations) of intention you planted (unconsciously or not) are starting to bloom. The full moon is a time to help us to remove anything negative, becoming fresh and renewed for the new moon phase ahead.

The moon phases serve as a spiritual tool to help let go of the old and make way for the new. Practising meditation at the full moon allows you to tap into the powerful natural energy source. It's also an excellent time to release all negative thoughts and emotions that can prevent you from moving on to a more fulfilled life and manifesting your dreams and aspirations. Emotions need to be expressed and released to be processed, the aim is to move the energy of emotion through and out of the body so we can let it go; doing this on a full moon is the perfect time to release.

The full moon is all about releasing anything we are holding onto that we no longer need; all negative emotions, anxiety, worries, stress, anything that's bothering us, past mistakes, burdens we are holding onto, just releasing it and letting it go. This will help us to end the cycle so we can be stronger, healthier, happier, and go into the next chapter, the new moon phase feeling renewed, refreshed and ready for bringing what we want to us. With this higher energy you may notice stronger psychic abilities and be able to connect stronger with your clairvoyancy.

I have seen various moon rituals being carried out on full and new moon cycles. Some full moon ritual examples:

- Write down everything you want to let go of, think about what is weighing you down, what you want to change, journal it all down. Perhaps put on some meditative music, light a candle, burn some incense and think about each item you are wanting to release to the Universe. When you are done, read your list out loud and feel the release as you burn the paper (safely, of course) and let those negativities be released to the Universe. Be warned, this can often be an emotional ritual, especially with our heightened full moon emotions!
- Meditate – create a sacred space or even better do a meditation outside under the full moon. Do a releasing full moon meditation, let go of what no longer serves you.
- Forgiveness – forgive others and forgive yourself for

anything they or you may have said or done. This is another way of releasing and letting those negative emotions and thoughts go. Think of what you want to forgive and say the words "I forgive".

- Create moon water – fill up a bottle of water and leave on your windowsill to charge with the moon's energy, even better put in a crystal, remember to research the best ones to use, as some minerals aren't consumable! Rose Quartz is a good one to use. You can drink the water infused with the moon's energy.

- Bathe in the full moon light. Energise and cleanse your body and mind by standing under the full moon; again you could do some meditation while you bask in its light and feel it encasing your body with its powerful, spiritual energy.

Try this meditation at the full moon.

Meditation for the Full Moon

Close your eyes and begin to feel your breath for a few counts, then take a deep breath in to open and expand you, and, as you breathe out, release a soft, easy breath, letting go of any tension, relaxing your mind (do this three times). Settling into a relaxed presence of calm and stillness, feel the breath flowing in and out, just be at ease following each breath you take.

Now picture the big beautiful full moon in the sky above you, the sky is clear, you can see the moon clearly. Breathe in the calm and joy from the moon's energy as it shines down over you, beaming down its energy, encasing you with a glow of pure lunar light energy. Breathe in the moon's powerful energy.

Imagine yourself connecting with Earth's energy below you, feeling your roots grounding you into the Earth.

Open up your right hand over your knee, palm facing up, to create a pathway to receive the moon's energy in your right palm and place your left palm on your left knee, facing down to pass down the energy. Creating a flow of energy, bring in the moon's cleansing energy in through the right palm, through the body and down and out through your left hand. Feel the moon's healing energy flow through your body and out of the left hand. Continue breathing into this cycle, letting the healing energy filter through your entire body as it nurtures, comforts, heals and soothes you.

It's time to let go now, you can release anything negative that you need to let go of; any past mistakes, negative feelings, emotions or burdens you're holding onto.

Breathe in the moonlight and let it go on the release of the breath, blowing the breath out and away as you release all the thoughts, all the tension, all the pain, all the emotions, letting them all go on every outbreath.

Repeat the affirmation, "I release you under the light of this full moon. I no longer need what does not serve or empower me."

Happy Full Moon Blessings.

New Moon

Day one to three is the new moon cycle, which brings us energy for creating our vision.

Representing birth and new beginnings, the new moon is a time to make 'wishes', setting your intentions for the month ahead, or even for the year! This is the perfect time for self-reflection, goal setting and starting new projects. It's time to think about your future, what do you want in life? Where do you see yourself? What goals do you want to set? It could be an imminent goal or something over the next six months to two years. You need to release your doubts around not being able to achieve and jump right into the possibilities of everything being available to you. Don't focus on the hows (how will I get this?), just believe it will be and there is enough for everyone. Being in a positive mindset to bring more positivity to you helps manifest your desires.

New Moon Rituals

The new moon is the time where you should be taking some time out for yourself for manifesting. Start by releasing what you don't need in your life, like at the full moon, take some time out to reflect and release, making way for new beginnings. On the new moon day, have a think about what you want, how you want to shape your life. It could be that you want to manifest a physical object; a car, a house, or it could be how you want to feel; how do you want to feel in your relationships with others? You may want to look at what you want for your family, your health, your wealth/finances, your career, what you want each day to be like. It's all about visualising those intentions, imagine they are already real, feeling them. This is really important in helping your intentions to manifest.

For example, you may want your dream job, imagine applying, imagine the interview going well, imagine receiving the phone call saying you have been successful and have been appointed for the job, feel those feelings of joy that brings you. Imagine being at your job, at your desk, meeting your new colleagues and being happy there.

- Perhaps put on some meditative music, light a candle, burn some incense and create a sacred space. Practice some gratitude first to shift you into manifesting mode.
- Put your wishes/intentions/goals in writing or even

draw them. As you do, see it in your vision, feel it within you as if it's real and has already come into fruition, enjoy the positive feelings it brings you, smile.

- Sit out underneath the new moon and meditate on your intentions, imagine sending your desire off into the Universe.
- You can either burn your list (safely, of course) as you see the smoke rising up to the Universe, taking care of your wishes/intentions, or keep your notes to refer back to over the upcoming weeks/months, keeping that positive energy flowing every time you read them.

Meditation for the New Moon

Begin to be aware of your breath, the gentle flow coming inwards and outwards. Rest a hand on each knee with your palms facing upwards, your thumb and first finger touching in Jnana Mudra. Trace the breath in and out, feeling a relaxation over you.

Invite the energy of the new moon to balance you. This new start, new chapter of life, feel it around you, absorb it, embracing the energy, welcoming in new beginnings, and connecting with the cycle of endings. Maybe you've just ended one chapter of your life, and this is an ideal opportunity to open the door, getting ready to step into your next chapter. Take in some deep breaths, absorbing this new moon energy, welcoming in the energy of the new moon and all the possibilities it can bring.

Be grateful for what you already have, what are you grateful for right now? Perhaps it's a physical object, perhaps it's an emotion, perhaps it's being grateful for the people in your life, the house you have, your career, your friends, family, your health, this day, this meditation, this time out. What are you grateful for?

As we give thanks to everything that surrounds our life, everything we have, everything we feel, we enter this new moon phase with gratitude.

Take a deep breath in and exhale out through the mouth; repeat three times.

The new moon's energy is bringing us new beginnings, the start of a fresh new cycle, as you repeat the mantra, "I am worthy," feeling the mantra and saying it out loud or in your mind: "I am worthy."

Welcoming the new moon cycle, what do want it to bring? Think now about one thing that you'd like to bring into your life, take a moment to think about what it is and why you want to bring this into your life. How will it make you feel if you had this in your life? Without thinking about how it will manifest, just trust the Universe will bring it into your life. Let these intentions seep into your body. Feel yourself smiling. Feel those feelings of what your wish will bring you when you receive it, does it bring joy, positivity, laugher, love, security? Whatever it is, go fully into the feeling it brings.

Breathe in deeply and fully exhale. Trust that the Universe is showing you the path and inspiring you in every moment, as you say the mantra, "I manifest what is best for the good of all, I manifest all I need with ease, I am aligned with the Universe."

Breathe in deeply and fully exhale as you visualise the white light of lunar moon energy shine down upon you, feel it radiating through and around your whole body, as you glow with this white lunar light.

Happy New Moon Blessings.

If you want to continue looking into moon cycles, I'd recommend looking into your horoscope and the zodiac signs that the new and full moon fall into. Yasmin Boland has a great book for this called *Moonology*. Also, mark in your diary when the new and full moons are occurring for the year so you can prepare!

CHAPTER 13

Other Holistic Practices

Reiki

Reiki comes from an Eastern tradition of energy healing; the word comes from the Japanese word's 'rei' meaning universal, and 'ki' which means life force energy that flows through all living things. This is a similar practice to crystal healing, using your hands to facilitate and channel healing energy to another. Reiki can also include crystal healing, using crystals as tools to amplify this energy. If we think of our bodies as an energy field, when our energy becomes out of alignment, and our vibration is out of tune, we manifest illness within the physical body, emotional unbalance, stress, tension, pain. Energy healing, including reiki, helps to realign and harmonise the energy to bring us into balance, our natural state, like resetting the clock. During a reiki session, the client will lie down for between 30-90 minutes, and the practitioner will place their hands lightly on and above the client using hand sequences. Sessions can help reduce pain, balance the energy, reduce stress and anxiety. Special reiki symbols can be used for protection and healing, by visualising, saying out loud or drawing them, as well as using intention to enhance and manipulate the flow of energy. You can send reiki healing energy to a person, or to a situation or future event to bring peace and calming vibrations.

Usui reiki is the most popular form of reiki, however there are lots of different stems. It is taught from Japan by Makao Usui, who is credited as the founder of modern reiki.

The transmission of this energy comes via a reiki teacher or master who creates the alignment within the practitioner. Reiki can be used to help to heal the mind, body and soul, helping to shift energy and heal the person with physical, emotional and mental ailments by creating a healthy flow of energy throughout the body.

Sound Healing

Music is known to help boost morale, soothe the mind, improve memory and cognitive function, help with relaxation and can lower stress and anxieties. A song that makes you feel good can be incredibly soothing for the body, mind and soul.

Sound healing therapy uses sounds from instruments played in a therapeutic way to rebalance the energy around and within the body and create relaxation and a calm space. Instruments can include things such as tingshas, singing bowls, tuning forks, gongs, chimes, and other musical instruments. These instruments create vibrations that help to balance the energy, through every cell in the body. The body is made up of 70% water, so each wave and vibration shared from the instrument flows through the body, creating a ripple effect, which helps to release energetic blockages. These vibrations rebalance the nervous system, boost the immune system and balance the left and right hemispheres of the brain to create a state of calm, soothing the mind, body and spirit, supporting emotional health and wellness. Sound healing sessions are beautiful deeply relaxing sessions, a great way to relax, easing stress and anxiety and even easing pain and lowering blood pressure.

Sound healing has been utilised across many cultures over thousands of years to balance energy. We know, dating back 40,000 years to the Australian Aborigines, that they used the didgeridoo as a healing tool. There is also knowledge of sound healing being used in ancient Greece to cure mental disorders. Hindis used mantras. Pythagoras was the first person to prescribe music as medicine, he used harmonic ratios as a medicine for diseases of the body, emotions and the soul, performing what he called 'soul adjustments'.

Sound can be used to help facilitate shifts in our brainwave state by providing a stable frequency, which the brainwave attunes to. We can shift from beta state, our normal waking consciousness, to alpha state, the relaxed consciousness. During deep relaxation, you can even shift into theta, which is a meditative state.

I enjoy using Tibetan singing bowls, which are placed on or around the physical body to create the vibrational waves, which travel through and around the body, bringing the body back into a state of harmony.

Tuning forks can be used to create the specific vibrational frequency and are placed onto the body to 'tune' in the frequency throughout the entire body, helping to rid 'blockages' of energy.

Shamanism

Shamanism is an ancient healing tradition. The word derives from the Tungus tribe in Siberia 'saman', sa meaning 'to know', so it translates to 'he who knows'. Dictionary. com describes a shaman as being, "A person who acts as an intermediary between the natural and supernatural worlds, using magic to cure illness, foretell the future, control spiritual forces, etc."

Although today practices have been distorted from the original traditional shamans, it is becoming more prevalent across the Western cultures. There are also different cultures of shamanism. It is common among the American Indians, Australian Aborigines and African groups such as the San.

Shamanic practices include connection with nature – why and how we came to be, healing those who are sick, following spiritual practices and being religious leaders, connection to the spirit world, escorting souls of the dead to the after world, and connecting with sacred places. It is believed they achieve a spiritual connection with themselves and the dead via a trance-like state.

Shamans, like other spiritual beings, will live their life in a true and respectful manner, connecting with the Earth and all natural places; lakes, waterfalls, sea, sand, Earth, developing their clairvoyant and healing abilities.

Shamans carry out ceremonies, which are a time for the community to come together and connect to the spirit world and themselves, bridging the two worlds, finding a connection and stepping fully into their highest expression of being. It is also a time for prayer, sending out your intentions to a higher source of power. For many shamans, prayer is more than just words, it's a way of life. Rituals are performed during ceremonies, sage can be used and words, sound and chanting, as people connect to nature, heal their wounds (physically and emotionally) and connect to spirit.

Yoga

Some people don't see yoga as being spiritual, but in fact yoga has lots of spiritual aspects. Not only is it great for stretching your muscles and increasing flexibility and balance, it's also rooted with spiritual aspects. Yoga originates from ancient India and its original purpose was to train the body and mind to become self-aware through spiritual development.

It enhances a mind, body and spirit integration. Yoga is a mindfulness practice, being aware of each movement you make, with conscious breathing, you remember your essential spiritual nature, letting go of the mind and being carefree and also finding that inner connection with yourself. It often involves meditation at the end of a session as you settle into a state of calmness and awareness of the body.

The poses in yoga are associated with animals, plants and nature and have a deeper meaning. For example, the lotus pose, which is a seated meditation position, is associated with the lotus plant; having roots underneath to ground you and the top half opening up like the petals to the divine. It represents divine birth and spiritual development.

The tree pose creates balance in the body and mind, with one foot rooted into the ground and the other on the opposite inner thigh, creating the symbol of a tree.

The warrior pose gives the idea of feeling courageous, bravery and strength to face your inner daemons and overcoming ego, with your legs rooted into the ground and arms powerfully extended.

Yoga is a beautiful art form, not only gaining strength on the outside in the physical body, but rootedness, strength and inner peace on the inside.

Smudging

Saging or smudging is an ancient spiritual ritual. It is derived from the Native American culture, but many cultures use sage for cleansing and getting rid of negative energies. I have previously mentioned smudging in the crystal section, it is a great way to cleanse crystals, but not only that, it is a great way to cleanse yourself, your home and environment (even your kids or partner!). Salvia officinalis is one of the most commonly used herbs in traditional medicine, known as 'sage', it is antimicrobial, which means it exhibits antibacterial, antifungal properties. Dried sage can be found in holistic shops (and my shop!). There are different varieties, but I tend to use white

Californian sage. It's usually bundled together and tied with string.

Smudging can help to get rid of negative energies within the home; it's not always about getting rid of spirits, which is what you've probably heard before. Although, this is still used for such process. If you move into a new home, the previous occupants' energy may be felt around the house. I highly recommend smudging any new place you frequent. When your sage arrives, burn the end until it starts to smoulder; you can then waft the smoke with your arm in a clockwise direction and go around each room in your home. You could also use a feather to help distribute the smoke. Ensure you go right into the corners of every room. While you smudge, you can say a mantra, for example, "May all negative energies be dispelled, and peace and harmony be restored."

You can cleanse your own aura with sage too. Simply light it as mentioned above and move your hand around your body. I tend to circle around so the smoke is in front and behind me to cleanse my energy field.

I always light sage and cleanse my healing room before and after clients; not only does it help get rid of any negative energies, it also helps to create a calm and peaceful setting. There are research reports that suggest that burning sage can lift your mood and reduce stress.

I do hope you have enjoyed finding an insight into spirituality and I wish you love, peace and harmony on your spiritual journey ahead. Remember, you don't *have* to practise all these techniques to be spiritual. This book shows some of the practices and ways of life you can take on board and gives you some direction to be able to delve deeper into your preferred methods at your leisure. I hope this has given you the inspiration you need to lead a peaceful, centred, spiritual way of life. I wish you well on your journey ahead, my friend. Find your inner self and manifest your greatest you!

Peace, Love and Light,

Sheryl

www.spiritualdreamscrystals.co.uk

Facebook & Instagram – Spiritual Dreams Crystals

spiritualdreamscrystals@gmail.com

Definitions

The Cambridge Dictionary defines 'spirituality' as: "The quality that involves deep feelings and beliefs of a religious nature, rather than the physical parts of life."

However, religion and spirituality do not always go hand in hand, doctrine can detract from the essence of spirituality. You do not have to be religious to be spiritual.

Wikipedia tells me that, "Spiritual but not religious", also known as, "Spiritual but not affiliated", is a popular phrase and used to self-identify a life of spirituality that does not regard organised religion as the sole or most valuable means of furthering spiritual growth.

So, in all essence, yes you can identify as spiritual or both religious and spiritual. Religion is more of a specific set of organised beliefs and practices, usually shared and practised by a community or group, whereas spirituality is more of an individual practice, the belief of there being something greater and having an understanding of life's greater purpose. With the new age movement, spirituality includes things such as healing, mediumship, astrology, moon phases, the paranormal and everything that is not physical, and also can include meditation, yoga and spiritual awakening.

References

I have been looking into different spiritual practices for many years, gaining knowledge and understanding from a range of sources. Below are references of spiritual teachers and practitioners who I resonated with:

Yasmin Boland – Astrologer and Moonologer (Author of *Moonology*)

Rhonda Byrne – Television writer and producer (Author of *The Secret*)

Esther (and Jerry) Hicks – Inspirational speaker, and author – Law of Attraction

Deepak Chopra – Indian-born American author and alternative medicine advocate

Donna Eden – Spokesperson for energy healing – https://edenenergymedicine.com/

Gabby Bernstein – Author, motivational speaker, spiritual

leader (Author of *Super Attractor*)

Michael Newton – Author (*Journey of Souls*)

Russell Brand – English comedian, actor, radio host, author and YouTuber

Biofield Study – https://www.ncbi.nlm.nih.gov/pmc/articles/PMC4147026/

Vex King – social media influencer, writer, mind coach and lifestyle entrepreneur (Author of *Good Vibes, Good Life*)

Ross Bartlett – Medium (Author of *Earth Angel*)

Hibiscus Moon – Crystal author, teacher and founder of Hibiscus Moon Crystal Academy. A former National Board certified professional science teacher with a Master's of Science (merging geology with curriculum, instruction and technology)

Eckhart Tolle – Spiritual teacher and self-help author

Journal

Please use this space to start your journaling journey! Use the headings as a prompt.

Positive affirmations I can use which resonate with me...

_____

_____

_____

_____

_____

_____

_____

_____

_____

_____

_____

_____

Positive Affirmations…

_____

_____

_____

_____

_____

_____

_____

_____

_____

_____

_____

_____

_____

_____

_____

_____

_____

_____

_____

_____

_____

_____

_____

What am I grateful for in my life and why…

_____

_____

_____

_____

_____

_____

_____

_____

_____

_____

_____

_____

_____

_____

_____

_____

_____

_____

_____

_____

Gratitude...

_____

_____

_____

_____

_____

_____

_____

_____

_____

_____

_____

_____

_____

_____

_____

_____

_____

_____

_____

_____

_____

_____

_____

_____

_____

New and Full Moon

As the new and full moon occur roughly once per month, use this space to note your monthly new moon wishes and full moon releasing. I have included twelve spaces for each month.

New Moon Month 1:   Date:

Work/Career	Relationships
Physical Objects	Emotions
Health	Finance
Monthly Overview	

Full Moon Month 1:

What do you want to release, what do you need to offer forgiveness for?

Release	Forgive

New Moon Month 2:   Date:

Work/Career	Relationships
Physical Objects	Emotions
Health	Finance
Monthly Overview	

Full Moon Month 2:

What do you want to release, what do you need to offer forgiveness for?

Release	Forgive

New Moon Month 3:   Date:

Work/Career	Relationships
Physical Objects	Emotions
Health	Finance
Monthly Overview	

Full Moon Month 3:

What do you want to release, what do you need to offer forgiveness for?

Release	Forgive

New Moon Month 4:   Date:

Work/Career	Relationships
Physical Objects	Emotions
Health	Finance
Monthly Overview	

Full Moon Month 4:

What do you want to release, what do you need to offer forgiveness for?

Release	Forgive

New Moon Month 5:   Date:

Work/Career	Relationships
Physical Objects	Emotions
Health	Finance
Monthly Overview	

Full Moon Month 5:

What do you want to release, what do you need to offer forgiveness for?

Release	Forgive

New Moon Month 6:   Date:

Work/Career	Relationships
Physical Objects	Emotions
Health	Finance
Monthly Overview	

Full Moon Month 6:

What do you want to release, what do you need to offer forgiveness for?

Release	Forgive

New Moon Month 7:   Date:

Work/Career	Relationships
Physical Objects	Emotions
Health	Finance
Monthly Overview	

Full Moon Month 7:

What do you want to release, what do you need to offer forgiveness for?

Release	Forgive

New Moon Month 8:   Date:

Work/Career	Relationships
Physical Objects	Emotions
Health	Finance
Monthly Overview	

Full Moon Month 8:

What do you want to release, what do you need to offer forgiveness for?

Release	Forgive

New Moon Month 9:   Date:

Work/Career	Relationships
Physical Objects	Emotions
Health	Finance
Monthly Overview	

Full Moon Month 9:

What do you want to release, what do you need to offer forgiveness for?

Release	Forgive

New Moon Month 10:   Date:

Work/Career	Relationships
Physical Objects	Emotions
Health	Finance
Monthly Overview	

Full Moon Month 10:

What do you want to release, what do you need to offer forgiveness for?

Release	Forgive

New Moon Month 11:   Date:

Work/Career	Relationships
Physical Objects	Emotions
Health	Finance
Monthly Overview	

Full Moon Month 11:

What do you want to release, what do you need to offer forgiveness for?

Release	Forgive

New Moon Month 12:   Date:

Work/Career	Relationships
Physical Objects	Emotions
Health	Finance
Monthly Overview	

Full Moon Month 12:

What do you want to release, what do you need to offer forgiveness for?

Release	Forgive

Printed in Great Britain
by Amazon

43894915R00106